GETTING THINGS DONE

Keys to a Well Balanced Life.

Insight Publishing
Sevierville, Tennessee

GETTING THINGS DONE

Published by Insight Publishing Company
647 Wall Street
Sevierville, Tennessee 37862

Interior formatting and design: Brittany Stewart
Cover Graphic Design: Emmy Shubert
Editor: Sandra Pinkoski

10 9 8 7 6 5 4 3 2

Printed in the United States of America

ISBN-10: 1-60013-200-6
ISBN-13: 978-1-60013-200-1

Table of Contents

A Message from the Publisher

Being able to get things done is about more than being an efficient, industrious self-starter. It includes being organized—mentally and in the workplace. It's about emptying your inbox, getting control of your schedule, and accomplishing your tasks.

I wondered how the busy, successful people I knew were able to get things done and I began to search for some answers. The result is this book and you will see why these men and women were asked to share their secrets.

I asked questions like, "What keeps you focused?" "How do you think technology factors into the theme of getting things done?" "What are the key areas of your plan that you consider in order to effectively manage life and work?" and I received some very interesting and informative answers. I think you'll agree.

When you read this book and incorporate the tools these authors have used to get things done, you'll wonder how you ever got along without them. The ideas you'll gain from this educational collection of interviews will help move you forward and enable you to take control of your work life and your personal life. If you need that extra bit of encouragement, that one piece of the puzzle to help you get things done in your own life, this is the book for you.

Wait no longer—turn the page and start your journey. You'll be glad you did!

Interviews conducted by:
David E. Wright
President, International Speakers Network

Chapter 1

Maurice Ramirez, CMO

David Wright (Wright)

Dr. Maurice A. Ramirez grew up in the south where the motivational admonishment of the day was, "If you can't run with the big dogs, don't get off the porch!"

Dr. Ramirez has been running with the big dogs ever since. He studied martial arts and Eastern philosophy since age five, he began programming mainframe computers at age sixteen, raised two daughters while a single parent in medical school, and he holds more board certifications than any other living physician. Dr. Ramirez co-founded a national professional organization for disaster medicine called The Disaster Life Support of North America. He runs a growing software company putting medical records in the patients' hands, and he owns a national training company dedicated to disaster preparedness. Dr. Ramirez travels the country as a professional speaker and celebrity expert; he even graduated from Clown College—despite failing juggling three times.

Dr. Ramirez uses his body, mind, relationships, and beliefs to balance a life and lifestyle that most only dream of. This rich wealth of knowledge, experience, and enlightenment illuminates a path for everyone who chooses to "get off the porch" and run!

Dr. Ramirez, welcome to *Getting Things Done: Keys to a Well Balanced Life.*

Dr. Maurice Ramirez

Thank you. How are you today?

Wright

Fine—it is a great day here in Tennessee.

Ramirez

Here in Florida as well.

Wright

What is *Bathtub Resilience*?

Ramirez

Bathtub Resilience is a concept that grew out of a survival skill that we have here in the hurricane belt. When a major storm is approaching, we encourage people to fill their bathtubs with water, just in case city services should fail. Here in Florida we have forty-thousand-gallon bathtubs. We call them swimming pools.

As I began teaching resilience and balance lifestyles around the country, the "40,000 Gallon Bathtub" became a metaphor for the resilience we have after a hurricane because we fill our bathtub before the storm, whether it is an eighty-gallon bathtub or a forty-thousand-gallon swimming pool. We then draw from that resilience to get us through those periods when life isn't so good. The air conditioning may be out, the power may out, but we don't go thirsty because we have a bathtub full of water.

Wright

How many forms of resilience are there?

Ramirez

We generally describe four types of resilience:

Physical resilience—the physical ability to get yourself through a difficult period of time. This comes both from your physical state of health as well as things you keep in reserve—dollars, food, and even water—in the event of a physical problem.

Emotional resilience—the strength we gain through our own experiences and relationships.

Relationship resilience—one of two forms of resilience that you can actually draw on from other people and share with others in such a way that two people rebuild and refill other areas between themselves.

Spiritual resilience—our belief in something beyond ourselves and the strength that belief gives us.

Wright

What constitutes "Physical Resilience"?

Ramirez

Physical resilience is exactly what it says--the state of our physical health and those things we do to maintain that health: eat a balanced diet, exercise, get enough sleep, as well as some of the physical things that we need to make life a little easier. Sometimes some of the physical things we need are just necessary such as taking our medications. You would be surprised to know how many people just won't take their medication. They are impacting their physical resilience. Even fiscal responsibility, making certain that our wants don't exceed our wallets, contributes to our physical resilience. Physical resilience means we maintain a certain physical responsibility with ourselves as well as a certain financial reserve for bad times.

Imagine being fifty pounds overweight, woefully out of shape, and recently discharged from intensive care after suffering an infection that devastated your liver and kidneys. You've regained your physical health through the skill of your doctors and nurses, but you can barely walk across the room. You are beyond couch potato—you're Jabba the Hutt!

This was my exact situation after a simple case of salmonella food poisoning that resulted in severe dehydration and hepatorenal failure. In essence, my liver and kidneys had all but shut down and my body spent two weeks using not fat, but muscle as its primary fuel source. While I had lost fifteen pounds, I had not lost more than a pound or two of my excess fifty pounds of fat.

I had been a competitive swimmer in my youth as well as a competitive martial artist while in medical school. I had intended to begin exercising after the first of the year. The holidays had not yet passed, but it was clear that I had to do something to regain even the barest minimum of physical strength and stamina.

Imagine jumping into your 40,000-gallon bathtub in December— literally. Even in Florida, and even in a heated pool, it is a shock. Fortunately fat floats, so my risk of drowning was low. The first few strokes were incredibly painful. Not only had I not exercised at all during my extended illness, but also these were muscles I hadn't used to any great extent in decades. By the time I had swum the 200 yards it took me to warm up I was physically exhausted and panting like a greyhound after a race. By 400 yards my now warm limbs were screaming and my face was hot and flushed. I could almost feel steam rising from my body even while I was in the water. By 500 yards I called it quits for the day.

Not much of a story on physical resilience except that the next day I got back in the water and again the day after that and the day after that. By February I was swimming two miles three times a week. I had lost thirty-five pounds of weight and an estimated forty-five pounds of fat. My muscle mass was up and at the end of two miles I was not breathing any harder than when I entered the water. My kidney and liver function were back to normal and I was in the best shape that I had been in since medical school.

Physical resilience is about dedication to repeated practice, to education, to creating resources needed for any event or situation.

Physical resilience is the development of perseverance through perseverance.

Wright

What constitutes "Emotional Resilience"?

Ramirez

Emotional resilience is that emotional strength—that emotional anchor—allowing us to weather life's storms when the tides are against us and the water is rising.

The best example of emotional resilience is found among children. Children can go through some of the most horrendous events in their lives—child abuse, school shootings, etc. and in a very short period of time (and yes, with some tears, consoling, and counseling), they come through just fine. As an emergency room physician, I have seen severely injured children come back two, three, four months later and they are just as happy and bubbly and laughing as though they'd not been injured. This is the tremendous emotional strength that we tend to forget as adults. We don't lose it as adults, but we lack it because we don't work to store up our emotional resilience, to cherish the special people and events in our lives.

Emotional resilience is the product of our own experiences. The unique thing about emotional resilience is that unlike physical resilience our experiences need not be the same as the adversity we now face.

Wright

What constitutes "Relationship Resilience"?

Ramirez

This is one of the greatest areas for us because this is one of the strengths that grow exponentially with every relationship we have.

Jim Cathcart, our lead author in this series, has a beautiful program in "Relationship Selling." It is based on the idea that the relationship is more important than the goal and that the relationship therefore serves the goal. In relationship resilience, that is exactly what we are talking about—not developing relationships for any other reason than the pure joy and strength that comes from having a connection with another human being. Everybody knows how bad a bad relationship can be. The flip side is that everybody knows how great that one super relationship in your life can be. Now imagine that greatness in every relationship you have.

Keeping the relationship canteen full is more than just accumulating friends and acquaintances. The relationship canteen is filled by the richness of those relationships and the connectedness created through friendships and family.

It is said that a person with friends is never truly alone and when your resilience is tested, a full relationship canteen is proof of that statement.

In my life I am fortunate to be blessed with a wonderful marriage. My wife, Laura, is intelligent, caring, compassionate, supportive, and beautiful. She is a fantastic mother and my best friend. Laura is absolutely supportive of me in everything that I do—not only my disaster response work but my everyday life, my beliefs (even when she disagrees with them), my dreams, my goals, and even my desires. Laura and I share a relationship that is special and, in modern society, increasingly rare.

Because I strive for physical preparedness both in body and in resources we maintain family preparedness in the same realms. We have a family plan in the event of an emergency and each of my children, as well as Laura, are well versed in every aspect of that plan. I know that I can count on Laura to keep the family safe no matter where I may go, what kind of disaster I respond to, what may befall them in my absence, or even in the event that I should never be able to return home.

When I must call upon my resilience, I have a full relationship canteen. Not only does my marital relationship contribute to this reserve—to this relationship resilience—but I have similar relationships with each of my four children and with my mother. What is more, even though my father is now deceased, my relationship with him remains a source of relationship resilience. I know that he is proud of me in the work that I do.

This limitless source of renewing strength ensures that I am able to endure and ultimately overcome any challenge ahead of me.

But again relationships are a two-edged sword when it comes to resilience.

Several years ago my younger daughter Tiffany suffered challenges of her own and I was away to assist in response and recovery for a declared national disaster. As a result of Tiffany's hospitalization my resilience was seriously compromised.

I was conflicted.

I was physically strong and physically prepared. I had all of the equipment and resources I needed to perform my disaster response duties. But the challenges facing somebody I cared about caused my relationship resilience to suffer significantly. Rather than being a source of strength, my need and desire to be home caring for my daughter sapped my strength. I was no longer sipping from my canteen of resilience. I was gulping deeply. My 40,000-gallon bathtub had sprung a leak!

The fact that I could do nothing, even if I were at her side, did not make a difference in how badly her needs affected my resilience. The fact that I would not even be allowed to be at her side during the first week of her hospitalization did not change the impact of her needs on my resilience.

Relationships are a two-edged sword for resilience but this does not mean that we should limit our relationships based on their potential impact. Quite to the contrary it means that we should expand our relationships—make them as deep and rich as possible and share in providing for the resilience of those we care about most deeply.

Wright

What constitutes "Spiritual Resilience"?

Ramirez

This is an area that has always been of great interest to philosophers throughout the ages. Your spirituality—your belief system—intersects with reality to create something almost magical in your life. We see this concept pop up over and over in society. The most current version of this is *The Secret,* but research has found that people who believe that they are not alone and that they are not disconnected from the rest of the universe live longer and survive adversity better than those who do not have such a belief. It doesn't matter *what* you believe, only *that* you believe. The fact is that belief improves health and likelihood of surviving an illness or injury. It improves the likelihood of success—the likelihood that you will actually achieve your goals.

Like emotional resilience, spiritual resilience grows when shared. But unlike all other canteens of resilience it is spiritual resilience that refills itself. Since we know that it does not matter in what we believe, but that we believe in some form of high order, high wisdom, or higher power—a "God" or guiding force in life. It makes sense that acting on our beliefs would add to our resilience.

It was spiritual resilience that sustained me during the multiple field response deployments of 2005. Hurricane Katrina was an absolute catastrophe in both a humanitarian and a physical nature. What the hurricane had not directly destroyed the levee breaches soon did. Lawlessness and anarchy brought a few to the baseness of human emotion and behavior. But the tragedy also brought out the best in many people. Like 9/11 before it, Hurricane Katrina's "ground zero" was dotted with signs that seem to reproduce like mushrooms, each one declaring "God bless New Orleans" or "we have faith, we will be saved."

These people not only publicized their beliefs (and their spiritual resilience), but they lived it. These individuals shared not only their stories with us as we treated their physical ailments, they told us that they would pray for us or that we were answers to their prayers. It is not unusual to receive perfunctory thank-yous in healthcare, but to be asked to pray with a group of survivors and then be the object of their prayerful thanks is both humbling and rejuvenating.

And for these wonderful survivors it was the act of expressing their spirituality that renewed them. Remember, this is New Orleans; we are not just talking Christianity, Islam, Judaism, but Sandinista and Voodoo—every form of religious expression, both familiar and exotic—and yet they all served a common end: they bound a people together and renewed them. The found the way to refill their own 40,000-gallon bathtub by pouring from their canteen of spiritual resilience.

It is this type of resilience that every business must have to handle catastrophic adversity. "Business Katrinas" fill the news almost every week and those affected are often left bereft of emotional resilience. The financial impact literally bankrupts their physical resilience. It is at these times that an abiding faith is imperative.

But faith in what?

In the 1980s the study of Sun Tzu and *The Art of War* introduced American executives to the concepts of balance and flow in battle and business. Sun Tzu wrote not only of strategy, but also of the need to understand one's place in one's world. More importantly, Sun Tzu emphasized planning with respect and consideration of the environment and the greater forces that determine the fate of our efforts. At the deepest level, *The Art of War* was about victory through surrender.

Wright

How do you build resilience? Let's start with physical.

Ramirez

Absolutely. Physical resilience is both the easiest to build and the hardest. The reason for that is we all know what we are supposed to do, but most of us don't want to do it. For the last two generations we have been told to eat a balanced diet. Once upon a time we had the food pyramid, it has been reshaped bit, but we basically know what a good meal is. Despite the fact that we know what a balanced diet is, most people in the United States don't eat a balanced diet.

Regarding exercise, we are not talking about those who are fortunate enough to have the time, energy, and the drive to run a marathon once a

9

week. We are talking more about getting thirty minutes of moderate exercise three times a week. A good brisk walk, a short thirty-minute swim, thirty minutes on an exercise bicycle is an achievable goal.

Then there is getting enough sleep. This is something we are really terrible about in the United States. The average American gets less than six hours of sleep a night and yet the average human being needs about seven to eight hours of sleep to really rejuvenate—to give their mind a chance to rest.

Finally, we cannot forget financial balance. We are a nation of debtors. We spend everything we earn and sometimes a little extra. That is something again that strikes at our physical resilience both directly and by adding stress.

Wright

What about emotional?

Ramirez

Emotional resilience is difficult for many people because it begins with the basic concept that I like myself. In fact, I must love myself and not in an egotistical fashion. I must see that I am the person I believe I should be and I like myself this way. I must accept that I therefore draw in and deserve all of the good things that come into my life.

I build emotional resilience by collecting those good things in my memory and in my heart. Sometimes there are bad things and I choose to learn through those rather than dwell on them as being some kind of punishment. Our nation was founded on puritan principles and while we are now the great melting pot and have many cultures and many religions, there is still a very real puritanistic belief that we are all are bad; that idea has to be let go. The whole idea of emotional resilience is that I deserve to be happy, I am happy most of the time, and the majority of people have good things happen in their lives most of the time. I must choose to focus on the good and pleasurable because that is what gives me strength for those short-lived times when things aren't going as well as I would like.

In the training environment, this type of "cross over" is exploited to help create emotional resilience in a number of professions. Airline pilots, the military, salespeople, law enforcement officers, and most recently, healthcare professionals, employ Immersion Simulation Environments to introduce controlled, simulated stress in a way that allows these professionals to develop emotional resilience.

The Internet abounds with software programs and even video games that allow a businessperson to "practice" their financial forecasting skills in their business management. Computer games and board games even provide an opportunity for emotional growth and the development of life skills.

But there is no "Flight Simulator" for life . . . or is there?

The "Flight Simulator" for life adversity and business adversity, however, is experience. The confidence that comes from encountering and overcoming the ebb and flow of daily life gently fills our canteen of emotional resilience. It is in the dealing with the burnt dinner, the flat tire, the person in the ten-item checkout line with twelve items, and the crying babies in the theater—they give us the opportunity to build our emotional resilience.

Whether or not we in fact use these "life lessons" to fill or drain our canteen is entirely our choice. We all know individuals who spend their lives complaining. Every little setback is a major problem, every challenge an insurmountable object. Some of these individuals, when faced with a truly tragic adverse life event, "rise to the occasion." Everyone around them is amazed that this individual is "managing so well." Unfortunately this is the rare outcome of failing to build emotional resilience from everyday life. In reality these individuals, when studied (and they have been), are really drawing their resilience from the other three canteens and in fact, most often from their spiritual canteen. When studied objectively it is often discovered that these individuals are emotionally overwrought or emotionally numbed. Their emotional canteen is bone dry and they are compensating from their other canteens.

On the other hand we all know people for whom life's little tragedies are nothing more than minor tribulations. These individuals are lights in the lives of their friends and colleagues. They are safe harbors when the emotional waters become stirred. They are often described with phrases such as "unflappable" or "steadfast," or "strong."

With these individuals, the trials of everyday life reassure them of their own strength and fill their emotional canteen.

It is not just our challenges that fill our canteen. While our relationships fill our relationship canteen, the emotions that our relationships create within us fill our emotional canteen. That is right—we get a two-for-one return on our investment. Even better, our emotional canteen is filled by the casual relationships we have at work. While is true that some of these work relationships fill our relationship canteen by being friendships as well, the encouraging pat on the back from a boss, the applause or accolades of colleagues, and even the comradery at the water cooler provides a sense of belonging and inclusion that quickly fills our emotional canteen to overflowing.

Our emotional canteen is also one of two that we can share with others. During times of adversity we can actually help fill another person's emotional canteen by sharing the life experiences and the feelings that surround those experiences with that other person.

The beauty of this ability to share emotional resilience is that it does not take even one drop from own canteen. In an almost miraculous fashion the sharing of the contents of our emotional canteen allows us to pour almost perpetually into the canteens of others and yet retain a full canteen for ourselves. It is not until we begin to sip or gulp from our own emotional reserve that we, ourselves, need to seek replenishment. Live richly, love honestly, and fill the canteen of emotional resilience.

Wright

And relationship resilience?

Ramirez

If relationships are to work, then relationship resilience is the payoff for that effort. The key to relationship resilience is to be connected. Emotional resilience relies on loving yourself. Relationship resilience relies on sharing yourself with the people around you. Relationship resilience comes from that interaction, from the joy of doing something together or sharing an experience or just spending time even without an activity. We live in a multitasking world now. "Multitasking" has become the phrase of the decade if not the millennium. Everyone wants to multitask and in a relationship sometimes the best time—the time that provides the greatest strength in a relationship—is spent just being still and quiet together. You may be part of a couple, together as a small group, or cheering with thousands of fans in a huge stadium. The relationships you build and that joint effort to a common goal provide relationship resilience. The relationship you build in a marriage or other significant relationship, relationships with children or grandchildren, friendships, and all nature of positive relationships make us stronger and more resilient every day.

Wright

And spiritual resilience? I would say it is different for everyone.

Ramirez

Everybody's experience in spirituality is different based on their chosen religion, but there are certain constants that differentiate those who believe in something outside of themselves from those who have no belief in anything outside themselves. Those who believe there is something beyond them retain a connection into a greater universe that the non-believe does not have. Fortunately most of us do believe in something greater than ourselves.

I think of these four forms of resilience like canteens. You fill all four of the canteens in the good times. You are going to drink from all four in the bad times. Three of the four (physical, emotional, and relationship) may run dry before the bad times pass, but spirituality refills itself because if you believe something is out there beyond yourself, there is always something to draw on. That 40,000-gallon bathtub is always there.

Wright

Wow, there's a lot more to resilience than I would have thought. Is there a single common "building block" for these four forms of resilience?

Ramirez

Yes, Father Robert Mitchell, a noted Catholic priest and philosopher once wrote of the difference between "like" and "love." Father Mitchell believes that "like" is an uncontrollable emotion, a reflexive response to our experience of another individual and the way we interact with them. According to Father Mitchell "liking" somebody or "disliking" them is as uncontrollable as the color of our eyes or the color of our hair.

"Love" on the other hand in Father Mitchell's world is a choice, an active decision based on the type of relationship we choose to have with another individual. Father Mitchell states that while we may respect some individuals very often we will neither like nor love them. Similarly Father Mitchell believes that there are many people who we like intrinsically. Our experience of them and our interactions with them lead us to the inevitable response of genuinely liking these people, yet we choice not to love them. As Father Mitchell states it is nice if we like them as well but we can choose to love somebody, in other words care for them as an individual and more importantly care what happens to them, even without respecting or liking them as a person.

It is this final paradox, loving without liking that Father Mitchell believes is the reason love is the ultimate "energizing" emotion. It is energizing because love is an active choice decision that we make to not only extend a relationship to someone else but to take control of ourselves and our lives. For Father Mitchell to love is the ultimate empowerment.

Another Catholic priest and philosopher, Father Dan Schulte, offered a functional definition of love:

"Love is a unifying response between two people who care for and have said 'Yes' to each others total being. It implies mutual respect, freedom and trust, and seeks the happiness and fulfillment of each other as a common goal."

For love to be the basic building block of resilience it must not only be a choice as Father Mitchell has stated but it must also fulfill all of the basic tenants of Father Schulte's definition.

"Love is a unifying response . . ."

In this phrase Father Schulte has encapsulates the most basic essence of the choice to love as well as its greatest hurdle. Love is a unifying response binding the person making the love decision to the person who is the recipient of that gift. It unites these two individuals creating something that is greater than the sum of its two parts.

". . . who care for and have said 'Yes' to each other's total being."

Father Schulte echoes Father Mitchell's sentiment that love here is a choice, a choice to accept ones partner in a relationship exactly as they are. No conditions, no qualifications, no equivocation.

It has been said that "no one self can see ones self through the eyes of another." If this is true then Father Schulte's definition holds that much more power as a building block of resilience. When we love another and enter into that "unifying" relationship we not only see ourselves as we are but find acceptance of ourselves as we are, not the way we wish we could be. It is through this acceptance that we can come first to respect ourselves then to like ourselves and finally we can make the active choice to love ourselves in the same way that we love others.

"It implies mutual respect, freedom and trust . . ."

Father Schulte emphasizes that the choice to love grows from the roots of respect. To love ourselves we must first respect ourselves. It is from this self-respect that Father Mitchell's emotional response to like ourselves springs. Similarly, since if we are to love another person we must first respect them. That respect grows from absolute and unconditional acceptance. Once respect is manifest it demonstrates itself through trust. Trust like love is an active decision. Paraphrasing Father Mitchell, "we do not choose to like, that is an uncontrollable emotional response. But we do choose to trust (love)."

". . . and seek the happiness and fulfillment of each other as a common goal."

Finally, Father Schulte reminds us that the choice to love is an active ongoing and demonstrative choice. We manifest this choice to love through the goals that we have for the relationship. If our goals for the relationship are completely focused upon ourselves then the relationship may represent respect and even like but it is clearly not love. It does not contribute to our resilience.

If, on the other hand, our goal of the relationship is strictly to please another person and does not include ourselves actively within the relationship then again it may represent respect and even like but it is not love. It does not contribute to our resilience.

For a relationship to actively demonstrate love it must balance our own self-interests with our desire to be selfless. If love is unifying response and therefore the love relationship becomes a true individual a sum of the two people who choose to share the relationship the contribution of love as a basic building block of resilience is that by choosing to create this love relationship we choose to create a reservoir of resilience for two.

The four forms of resilience are all based on this simple emotion, love. Whether it is our physical resilience, our emotional resilience, our relationship resilience, or our spiritual resilience each requires that we make the active decision to love in order to build that resilience, to fill that canteen. Simultaneously, we fill our forty thousand gallon bathtub of resilience with this basic element of resilience, love.

Wright

How did your own life experiences lead you to *Bathtub Resilience*?

Ramirez

Bathtub Resilience grew out of the reality of using our swimming pool as a source drinking water after Hurricane Charlie. I realized that not only was I drawing water for myself, but also for my mother and for neighbors, and that we were drawing from each other for relationship resilience and for emotional resilience. It just simply came together around the idea of a swimming pool full of resilience. Jokingly, a friend of mine said it sounded like a huge bathtub and from there the term "bathtub resilience" was coined.

Wright

Why create The Original My Medical Records Software?

Ramirez

Initially I was with the American Red Cross and I later became a disaster responder through varies medical organizations. I am now involved through the federal government. Mr. Goodman has been part of disaster community recovery for over thirty years, physically rebuilding devastated communities. We each saw over the course of our combined more than fifty years that society in general and people individually have become more and more reliant on technology as well as on the government. People have lost the basic ability to get through the first seventy-two hours. They've also lost their ability to relate simple medical information without accessing their pharmacy or medical records. It was shocking how many people would look at us and say, "I don't know" in New Orleans. They would ask us to call their pharmacist; unfortunately, the pharmacy was under water, gone forever. Out of that need came The Original My Medical Records.

Wright

Tell me more about "The Original My Medical Records."

Ramirez

Our CEO Arnie Goodman and I saw that both disaster victims and the general public needed the ability to carry with them their actual medical records. There are a number of products that do this out of the market. The Original My Medical Records is different in that it has the ability to store information that can be carried on your person as well as to interface with an actual medical record in a doctor's office or hospital

17

and synchronize and absorb the additional information so that your data is always current. It is carried in a USB flash drive device whether on a key ring or a watch. It is a way to add to your physical and emotional resilience.

Wright

Why give away this information and the software?

Ramirez

We are spending right around twenty thousand dollars to distribute all of this because we feel it is an absolute need. This is basic software. I wouldn't be honest if I said this is a full enterprise version of the software. It is a "Lite" version, it does everything all of the other programs on the market do, so for free you are getting software that would cost anywhere from seventy-nine to one hundred and nine dollars. Mr. Goodman feels this basic information should be in the hands of every person out there.

The "Lite" version was an in-house "proof of concept" program. The "Lite" version was one of the mileposts to get where we thought the full retail version of the software needed to be. After we spent all that money to develop it, Mr. Goodman decided that it would only cost a fraction to give it to the people who need it. There is a certain point where you build your relationships and build your resilience and this is how we want to express our resilience.

Wright

What an interesting conversation. Dr. Ramirez, I appreciate the time you have taken to answer these questions. I've learned a lot here and I know our readers will too.

We have been talking with Dr. Maurice Ramirez who runs a growing software company putting medical records in patients' hands. He also owns a national training company dedicated to disaster preparedness. Dr. Ramirez travels the country as a professional speaker and celebrity expert.

About the Author

In the wake of Hurricane's Katrina and Rita, and with concerns of pandemic influenza vibrating on the horizon, it is more evident than ever that we need to effectively organize our ability to conduct planning and coordinate our response for complex emergencies and disasters at every level of society.

For over two decades, Dr. Maurice Ramirez has taught captains of industry, physicians, residents and medical students how to make faster, better and more accurate decisions in every possible situation. Dr. Ramirez teaches corporate leaders and their organization to apply the Lessons Learned in the Disaster Field Office to Triage Decisions, make Instantaneous Assessments, avoid HMO (Heavily Mulled Over) decision paralysis, and practice their CPR (Complete Personal Resilience).

Dr. Ramirez has recently shared the platform with Speaker Newt Gingrich, Senator Robert Dole, Secretary of Health and Human Services, Tommy Thompson, and other dignitaries. Through his seminars, keynotes and consulting countless executives and physicians have learned the skills that save lives, and livelihoods.

Dr. Ramirez is board certified in multiple medical specialties. As a residency trainer, ER physician, author, researcher, and professional speaker he has been cited in over twenty textbooks with several chapters devoted exclusively to his work.

Dr. Maurice Ramirez
1200 Providence Rd.
Kissimmee, FL 34744
407.301.3458
renaissancedoc@mauricearamirez.com
www.MauriceARamirez.com

To Contact My Medical Records, LLC
Attn: Arnie Goodman, CEO
30799 Pinetree Rd.
Pepper Pike, OH 44124

Chapter 2

Jim Cathcart

David Wright (Wright)

Today we're talking with Jim Cathcart, CSP, CPAE. He is founder and president of Cathcart Institute, Inc., and an advisor to the Schools of Business at Pepperdine University and California Lutheran University. He is one of the most widely recognized professional speakers in the world. As the author of thirteen books and scores of recorded programs, his students number in the hundreds of thousands. He is a past president of the National Speakers Association (NSA), winner of the Cavett Award, member of the CPAE Speaker Hall of Fame, Certified Speaking Professional (CSP), a member of the exclusive Speakers Roundtable (twenty of the world's top speakers), and in the year 2001 he was a recipient of the Golden Gavel Award from Toastmasters International. Jim is an industry leader among speakers. He is also co-author of *Professional Speaker System*™ used by top professionals to grow their own speaking businesses and refine their skills. With over 2,500 professional speeches to his credit, Jim Cathcart is a true veteran of the platform with an active speaking calendar today.

Among professional speakers worldwide, Jim Cathcart is an Industry leader. He has risen to the top of his profession through thirty years of presentations to a worldwide audience and decades of unselfish service to his profession. He believes in serving his industry and community as well as his customers.

Jim, welcome to *Getting Things Done: Keys to a Well Balanced Life.*

Jim Cathcart (Cathcart)

Thank you very much; it's a delight to be aboard.

Wright

Jim, you've been referred to as a motivator, a visionary, and a pioneer in the speaking profession. Will you tell us how you came to earn this recognition?

Cathcart

I tell you, there's a long answer there! I've been referred to as a lot of unsavory things too, by neighbors and other people in traffic I'm sure.

Years ago I heard Earl Nightingale on the radio. He inspired me so much that I said, "That's what I want to do with my life!" I want to help people grow. So I set about learning personal development and being involved in the field of communication and leadership. I got really fanatical about it for about five years. Every day I would get up in the morning and I'd listen to a tape (or back in those days it was a record) and I'd be reading two or three books at a time. I'd go to every seminar I could find that dealt with aspects of motivation. I was really immersed in it. My son said that I ate, drank, and breathed motivation!

All my friends who were not interested in goal-setting and personal achievement and things of that nature drifted away and I found a new circle of friends. I learned more and more about this profession we're in today.

In 1976 I joined the National Speakers Association, which was a small group of less than two hundred speakers back then. Today it's comprised of 4,000 professional speakers around the country and around the world. They own their own conference center in Tempe, Arizona, and they have a foundation that gives away millions of dollars. It's phenomenal what has happened since those early days.

But for me it all started when I heard Earl Nightingale on the radio. I knew I want to do that.

Wright

You spoke of helping people grow. You're book, *The Acorn Principle,* is the product of your twenty-plus years of research in human performance. Will you explain to our readers what the principle is?

Cathcart

The Acorn Principle states that if you start with an acorn you will always get an oak! Even if you send the acorn to "Redwood Camp," acorns produce oaks 100 percent of the time—it's a slam-dunk. Now whether it's a mighty oak or a little scrub brush that dies prematurely depends on what you do with that acorn.

The same thing is true with the talents and abilities inside each person. You have a seed of potential that contains hundreds and perhaps thousands of possibilities that are available to you. But there are also hundreds and maybe thousands of possibilities that *aren't* particularly open to you. There are some things that if we try to do them, we'll almost never do them well, and there are things that if we try to do them, we'll do them magnificently!

So every person is suited for something and not suited for other things. It's just our nature. It doesn't mean we can't do particular things, it just means that we can't necessarily do it alone without resources and without other people, without a team, without software, or whatever kind of support might be available. So every person needs to listen to that little voice inside them that tells them what they love and what they like and what they enjoy and what makes them feel worthy and gives them a sense of fulfillment. That is the seed speaking to you and telling you, "This is what gives me joy, let's pursue this path." For some people it's building things, and for some it's working with numbers and figuring out solutions to problems, and for some it's nurturing and helping, for some it's selling, and for some it's managing. Everybody has their own talents and everybody needs to discover those talents and then nurture them. Instead of trying to become a spruce or an elm or a willow or something else, if you are an acorn you need to plan to become an oak.

Wright

One thing you specialize in is helping people to discover their priority values. It seems that in this country we have had a lot of problems with lack of a good set of values in leaders of our major corporations and in politics within the past few years. Will you tell us what values you teach?

Cathcart

There are common values that are part of everyone, and there are seven of them that I call Natural Values. These are values that are upheld regardless of your political affiliation, your race, your gender, or the country where you grew up. We have all these seven values. They are natural and they are a part of being human.

A "value" is something that is important. When you are comparing values you are talking about is the relative importance of this versus that. How important is having nurturing relationships versus getting recognition for a job well done? Both of those things are important, but it depends upon the situation and the person and a many other factors as to which one is *most* important today.

The Sensuality Value—the relative importance of your physical experience—is a big deal at certain times. An example is when you're really uncomfortable or in a position that if you continue to do whatever you're doing physically you might get injured. At that time you need to focus on the Sensuality Value over everything else. You focus on the Sensuality Value at that point in time to avoid injury or get yourself more comfortable so you can focus on something else.

You could probably do your work all day leaning across your desk and typing backwards, but *why*? The reason is because you'll be ten times as productive and a whole lot happier if you'd simply rearrange the desk so that you can sit comfortably and do your work. The Sensuality Value has its place.

Also, it relates to selling—if I'm selling to you and I understand from some of the comments you make that it really matters to you how the machine *feels* in your hands or how the clothing fits or how the chair fits the shape of your body or how the screen on your computer aligns with your natural line of sight, I can use that as a selling point. And if that's not important to you, then my using that as a selling point is just like my singing a song that you don't particularly enjoy and asking you to buy the record.

So that's the Sensuality Value.

The second value is Empathy, the ability to feel connected to people. There are some people whose entire life is driven by that value. When they get up in the morning they want to immediately start communicating with someone else and they've got a 100 percent tolerance for human contact. They don't want to disconnect until they are asleep again.

So it's a matter of how important that value is to you, how vital is it to feel connected to other people? If it's vital and I'm selling to you, then I'm going to talk about how this will affect your relationships, the people you care about, what the experience of buying from me will be like as it relates to you and the people you associate with, and how it's going to affect your employees and your family, etc.

Then you can see, once you understand that value exists, how it fits into the way you sell, the way you manage, the way you parent, and the way you choose your right priorities.

I use the letters in the acronym S-E-W- P-A-C-K as a memory tool to remember the seven values. If you think of those little sewing kits that are provided sometimes in hotel rooms that have five or six colors of thread and a needle and a button or two, that's a "Sew Pack."

Think of it as a way to weave together all these values: "S" for sensuality, "E" for empathy, "W" for wealth, "P" for power, "A" for aesthetics, "C" for commitment, and "K" for knowledge.

Sensuality—Sensuality is of relative importance to your physical experience.

Empathy—Empathy is the relative importance of feeling connected with other people.

Wealth—Wealth is the relative importance of ownership, of having things that are considered valuable.

Power—Power is the relative importance of getting recognition or being in control and running things.

Aesthetics—Aesthetics is the importance of how things look—beauty, balance, symmetry, blend, patterns, things of that nature. For some people, if their office is beautifully organized they do their work better. If a proposal comes to them and if it looks really neat and tidy and attractive, it's more likely to get their attention and be considered seriously than if it's sloppy or just stapled together in the corner. So aesthetics matters to some people sometimes more than it does to others.

Commitment—Commitment is the relative importance of doing the right thing, of being committed to a cause, to having some greater purpose bigger than you are that's driving and pulling you at the same time.

Knowledge—Knowledge is the relative importance of knowing and learning and discovering and understanding.

We could do a whole seminar on just those values and how they affect everything else you do. These values are a part of the book, *The Acorn Principle*.

Wright

I've got one employee in my office that I think reads everything you write. She was trying to explain to me the other day about your Mastery Grid. All I could get from her was something about purpose and contribution leading to fulfillment. Would you explain this to the readers a little bit?

Cathcart

You bet; this one's pretty quick and simple. It's something that I came up with in the 1980s and I've refined it ever since. Two things that make a difference in your life are how you think and what you do. If you change the way you think, you change your results. If you change what you do, you change your results. And if you work on both of them at the same time, or alternate working on them, then you get better even quicker! So someone whose thinking is very low level—very fundamental, "what you see is what you get," don't look beyond today, don't think beyond the moment—is not contributing much. People who think like that are like a machine—they are a "doer," they pull the lever on the machine and hand the ticket to somebody and that's about all they do. You could make another machine to do that for you. But if that person starts realizing his or purpose in, for instance, pulling a lever and handing a ticket to somebody is to cause the person to feel welcome and be excited about being there, then that person has added value to that experience.

To go deeper here, let's say it's a check-in booth at a movie theater. So you go up to the ticket booth and you give the person your money and tell him or her what movie you're seeing and you get your ticket. Well, that could have been done with a credit card and a machine; you didn't need a person in there. But, if that person selling tickets says, "Good evening! Welcome to United Theaters. What movie would you like to see?" and the person hands you a little coupon and tells you, "Here's a special discount on our large popcorn. I hope you enjoy your movie." The person in the ticket booth has now added *value* to that experience; it's not just a transaction that could have just as well been taken care of by a machine. It's an interaction with a person who has begun to make you feel a sense of hospitality. You look forward to the movie and you feel that this is "your" theater and you belong there, the workers there are people you know, they like you, it's good to be here, and you're not just buying a ticket to go into a room and see a movie.

We need to understand that the way we think affects the way we act. Let's say you're working for me, and you're a salesperson. If I can get you to realize that this is not about making sales but it's about helping people. The way we help people is by making sales; but if it's not appropriate to make a sale or if the customer is sincerely not interested in what you have and is not just brushing you off, then don't continue to try to sell because that will be offensive. You're not going to make the customer's life better. Even if you complete the sale the customer is going to feel exploited instead of served. So the job of a salesperson is to make the customer's life better and the way that is done is by helping the customer make a good buying decision.

If I have that kind of thinking going into a sales contract, my behavior will change. It will change from the old vendor mentality of just "close, close, close, close, close until they buy," to more of a provider and supporter mentality where I make a recommendation, we discuss it, I ask about the customer's needs—I collaborate with the customer to come to a buying decision.

The idea behind it all is that business ought to be an act of friendship—a profitable act of friendship. It ought to be profitable to me as the seller and it ought to be profitable to the customer as the buyer. So if the customer doesn't profit through the value of what I sell, then I shouldn't be selling to that customer, I should sell to someone else. If I don't profit through the sale of what I'm offering then I don't get to do it very long because I'm going to go bankrupt!

So the way we think and the way we act is important. You can work on people's actions and get them better at their jobs. You can work on their thinking and get them better at feeling a sense of purpose and meaning in what they do. And if you work on both of these actions alternately, not neglecting either one, then people move from victim mentality to leadership mentality and they realize how to make a difference. They will take initiative more often.

Wright

Your Behavioral Economics program says every action has a value or a cost. Is this true in personal life as well as professional?

Cathcart

The answer is yes, of course. But let's look at it. Every action has a value or a cost. Also, every attitude has a value or a cost. Let's say that I work for you and I believe that business is a bad thing. Somehow, from my parents or my leaders over the years, I got the attitude that businesspeople are bad people. If I believe that business is a bad thing, then I only work because I have to work and not because I want to work. And I'm going to feel "dirty" for doing it because I believe that what I am doing is a bad thing. Does that attitude have a cost? Absolutely! It would make me cynical and pessimistic, and it would cause me to feel bad about myself. I probably would not do my work very well. I'd call in sick more often, and I'd be more likely to take advantage of my employer and my customers; it's an ugly attitude.

Now, what if I believe business is the way that great people in society help each other? If I believe that business is a way that people in a free society help each other, then I look at every business as a potential benefit! And if I think that what they are doing is a noble thing, then I think that what I'm doing as a noble thing! I feel honorable in doing it, therefore I feel better about myself, I feel better toward my customer, and my work will be done better.

Now, do you think that will change the way I interact with my family and in the evening after work? Yes! So every attitude has a value or a cost that shows up not just on the job, but all throughout life. And every action has a value or a cost.

For example, what if every morning I turn off my alarm, set it on snooze, and let it go through its next cycle before it wakes me up again? If I let that happen every single morning, that would be my habit. That habit causes me to never be immediately responsive to an alarm so I'll tend to "drag" myself into each day and resent the first alarm because it bothered me and I'll wait for the second and maybe the third before I get up. In time maybe I'll even turn it off and end up showing up late for work or whatever I was going to be doing that day.

Little attitudes and little actions add up to bigger attitudes and bigger actions. For example, if I drank a glass of wine with dinner, it's no big deal. If I drink a glass and half of wine the second week, and then a month or two later I find I'm drinking two glasses of wine at dinner, then we are talking about a pattern of increasing alcohol consumption— deadly alcohol consumption. The odds are very good that if I don't do something to change the pattern, those two glasses of wine will become three and I'll have a drinking problem!

So you've got to helicopter up once in a while and look down at yourself and look at your patterns. See if you've picked up somebody else's wisecrack remark and if you're patterning what that person does and determine if the ultimate end of that pattern is a negative attitude for you.

For example, somebody says, "Good morning," and another person says, "Yeah, what's so darn good about it?" Some people think the remark is clever and they say it all the time. But if you think about it, that's a very ugly attitude. It can be cute if you do it once in awhile, but if you do it all the time you'll be perceived as having a sour attitude.

A friend of mine said that one day. I said, "Good morning," and he said, "What's so darn good about it?"

I stated, "I wasn't commenting on the morning, I was wishing you one—and I take it back!"

"What?" he asked.

"I'm not telling you what kind of a morning it is," I replied, "I was wishing you a good morning and I take it back."

"Well, don't take it back."

"Then," I said, "don't answer back in such a wisecrack way!"

"Well—okay," he said.

Wright

By using this plan of action, can you change someone else's behavior if it is adversely affecting your life?

Cathcart

I know you can! I've had years and years of experience watching others. If you become more aware of how your thoughts affect your life, know how your actions affect your life—the little ones as well as the large ones. We all know that robbing a bank is an ill-advised behavior, but cheating on the little things like the amount of change you give someone or when someone drops a dollar bill on the floor and you pocket it is being dishonest. We don't think of those things as nearly as important as robbing a bank because we know that robbing a bank will get us thrown in prison. Keeping that dollar bill might just get you into an argument with that person. But both of these actions can lead you to realizing that you are dishonest because if you behave dishonestly more than once, then you start becoming a dishonest person.

To become an *honest* person you break the pattern of dishonesty and you become scrupulously honest, meaning that you go out of your way to do the right thing even when it's not your responsibility to do it. So you can change by changing the little patterns. You have to make a commitment. You draw a line in the sand and say that from this point forward you're not going to do that anymore. If you catch yourself doing whatever it was, you stop yourself and correct it.

You can change you. I know it for a fact because I grew up expecting to lead a small unimportant life, but then I heard Earl Nightingale on the radio back in the 1970s and I said, "I can do what he said to do!" What he said was to spend an hour a day in study in your chosen field, and five years from now you will be a national expert in that field.

My chosen field was his field. I wanted to be an expert in human development—I want to help people grow—so I became fanatically dedicated to that for about five years. Sure enough, five years later I was full-time professional speaker and trainer. And now I have thirteen books in print, I've traveled the world, I've been president of my industry association, and I've spoken in every state in the nation! So I know that this stuff works.

When Earl Nightingale passed away, I was the only speaker at his memorial service besides his widow, Diana.

Now, when I first heard him on the radio I was a government clerk making five hundred bucks a month in Little Rock, Arkansas. I had no prospect of ever meeting or seeing Nightingale in person. The Nightingale Corporation, by the way, has recorded albums of me and has sold over three and a half million dollars worth of them. So that's how far it can go from just being an hourly worker who's an assistant in a government office listening to someone on the radio; no college degree, no money in the bank, no connections in the community.

Wright

Recently you and I had a conversation about Life Balance that really interested me. In the *Dynamics of Goal Setting,* Paul Meyer talks about the six areas of life—Financial, Physical, Mental, Family, Spiritual and Social. How do you balance all of these different areas in your life?

Cathcart

One of the things I do is similar to exercising muscles. If the only muscle you exercise is your right forearm, then you're going to look like the comic character Popeye attached to Olive Oyl—she was long and thin and skinny and he was all muscle. When it comes to your life, if all you're exercising is your career muscle, then your family muscle and the other parts of your life will be neglected. The degree to which you neglect one part of your life is pretty much equal to the degree to which that part of your life is going to later interrupt all the other parts of your life!

For example, if you don't take care of your physical health, your physical health will finally say, "My turn!" and you'll be sick for a long period of time, which interrupts everything else that you do. If you don't take care of your family and your relationships with your various family members, then sooner or later your relationships with your family are going to get in the way of your work, your social life, and a whole bunch of other things.

It's the same thing with personal finances and it's the same thing with your job. It's the same thing with your spiritual life and your sense of connection with God.

So all of these parts of you deserve their moment.

For people who never ever cry, they are not acknowledging or honoring that part of their emotions. There are plenty of moments in life when crying is the appropriate response. If you don't allow yourself to cry and if somehow you think you're being strong by not crying, then you're stifling part of your emotional language so to speak. And it's not good for you. It's not good for you physically, nor is it good for you psychologically.

I'm not saying that you should just blurt out and cry in the wrong situations, but there are times when it makes very good sense for you to nurture your soul and your spirit and grieve for a person or a thing or an experience that you had. Then likewise you want to have some times when you laugh so hard that you virtually bend yourself double. If you're not having a great laugh once in a while, it's a part of you that needs expression!

All of these are perfectly valid emotions and we ought to allow them out. Balancing your life is matter of alternating your attention between every one of the various parts of your life on a pretty regular basis so that there's never a long period of time when any part of you has gone neglected.

Wright

Les Brown states that *The Acorn Principle* guides us on a fascinating journey within. Brian Tracy, one of the greatest trainers alive today, says it explains perhaps the most important single principle you can ever learn to guarantee success, happiness, and lifelong prosperity. Pretty heavy words!

Cathcart

Thank you, yes. I've been fortunate to know and be friends with the top people in the field of personal development. And it's interesting that

33

that was my goal. When I decided to get into the field of personal development, I wanted to meet and hang around with the good guys! I wanted to know the people like Earl Nightingale and Zig Ziglar. Zig's a good friend, and Brian Tracy I've known and been friends with for years. Tony Alessandra and I were partners for a long time and we're still best friends. I've been hired by Ken Blanchard to speak to his own organization. I've been hired by Brian Tracy and Stephen Covey and others to speak to their organizations over the years, so it's been thrilling! These people are serious speakers; they don't take what they do lightly. They are deep and wide in their subject areas, and they are good people as well. They are the kind of people you can really enjoy being around socially or just casually. So when they've honored me with positive comments about *The Acorn Principle* it humbles my soul; at the same time it thrills my heart because it's such a wonderful thing.

Jack Canfield and Mark Victor Hansen, co-authors of the entire series, *Chicken Soup for the Soul,* which has sold a millions of books (beyond the wildest dreams of even some of the most successful publishers in the world), have been friends of mine for decades. I've known Mark since the 1970s and I've known Jack since the 1980s.

Wright

You lead a very active life in your professional and your personal life. What advice can you give our readers on juggling the different areas of their own lives to help them lead a better and more balanced life?

Cathcart

First you need to determine what you care about. This goes back to values. You don't look at the values; you look at what you care about. Then you compare that to values to see what the themes are, and that tells you about you. Get a copy of *The Acorn Principle* and read through it. Underline and highlight important points that stand out and ask yourself the questions at the back of each chapter. Look at the little things I call "thought breaks" throughout the book, which are little questions to ask yourself.

I believe that the first thing you've got to know is what you care about. And the second thing is: what do you want? Until you know what it is you want, it's hard to make a choice about what to do next and to set goals. It's hard to know what's going to help and what's going to hinder. So goal setting is a vital thing.

One very close friend of mine always seems to have a difficulty with goal setting and I asked her why, "What's the deal with you and goal setting?"

"I don't know," she replied. "It's just like I have to get an A. It's like an assignment or something, and if I don't get an excellent grade at my goal-setting and don't achieve the goal I'm a failure."

I asked her how she determines what she cares about, and she said that she likes to write out her dreams. That was interesting—she was talking about describing her dreams in writing; but if I called them "goals" she had a problem with it! Call them "dreams" and she has no problem with it at all. So that relates back to some experience in her own childhood I'm sure, where an authority figure made her feel oppressed related to study and academic achievement.

You need to get into a habit of writing down what you want. If you want to be in a position of authority or achieve something significant, if you want to see the great places in the world, if you want to be considered a solid citizen in your community, if you want to be a leader in your school district or an exceptionally good parent, or if you want to know for sure that you're one of the best friends that a person could have, whatever those goals are, write them down! A good way to stimulate goal setting is put what you want into categories. For example, use Paul Jay Meyer's model for goal setting. I use eight categories— mental, physical, family, social interactions with other people, spiritual, career, financial, and emotional as related to what brings me joy and happiness and a sense of fulfillment. So take each of those areas and write out your dreams.

Ask yourself, "If the world was perfect and I get to have everything I want or have everything or be everything that I want in all these areas, what would some of those things be?" Write it out and then date it.

Always date the piece of paper you're doing your goal setting on, and then when you come back and write on it some more write the new date there also. Then you can reflect back at what point you were in your life when you wanted to attain certain goals. For example, my goals back in the 1970s are quite different from my goals in the '80s or '90s or in 2000. I can look at the factors in my life and see a direct relationship in some cases between where I was in my career or what was going on in the world, or where I was in terms of age, etc. Was I single? Was I married? There are all kinds of things to look at.

In the book, *As a Man Thinketh* by James Allen (one of the classic inspirational works of all time), he says that the key to understanding the connection between thought and circumstance is to learn to monitor it and to look at it over time and connect how you were thinking and what you were doing and what kind of results you were getting at each point in your life. So it goes back to my Mastery Grid or Fulfillment Grid—do things that you can control, how you think, and what you do. And the more you are aware of what you think and what you do, the more you can take action to change how you think or what you do. And that will bring you the results you hope to achieve.

Wright

What a great conversation, Jim. I'm blessed that I get to talk with people like you!

Cathcart

Thank you, thank you—and you make for a stimulating conversation because you are interested in what I am interested in! So you help me bring out some of the best ideas I have, and I appreciate that!

Wright

Today we have been talking with Jim Cathcart, one of the most widely recognized professional speakers in the world. He is also author of thirteen books and scores of training programs. His students number in the hundreds of thousands.

Jim, thank you so much for taking all this time today to answer these questions. I really appreciate your participation in *Getting Things Done*!

Cathcart

You're very welcome, David. I enjoyed it thoroughly!

About the Author

JIM CATHCART, CSP, CPAE is founder and president of Cathcart Institute, Inc., and an advisor to the Schools of Business at Pepperdine University and California Lutheran University. He is one of the most widely recognized professional speakers in the world. As the author of thirteen books and scores of recorded programs, his students number in the hundreds of thousands. He is a past president of the National Speakers Association (NSA), winner of the Cavett Award, member of the CPAE Speaker Hall of Fame, Certified Speaking Professional (CSP), a member of the exclusive Speakers Roundtable (twenty of the world's top speakers), and in the year 2001 he was a recipient of the Golden Gavel Award from Toastmasters International.

Jim is an industry leader among speakers. He is also co-author of the *Professional Speaker System*™ used by top professionals to grow their own speaking businesses and refine their skills. With over 2,500 professional speeches to his credit, Jim Cathcart is a true veteran of the platform with an active speaking calendar today.

Among professional speakers worldwide, Jim Cathcart is an Industry leader. He has risen to the top of his profession through thirty years of presentations to a worldwide audience and decades of unselfish service to his profession. He believes in serving his industry and community as well as his customers.

Jim Cathcart
2324 Crombie Court
Lake Sherwood Forest, CA 91361
800.222.4883
info@cathcart.com
www.cathcart.com

Chapter 3

David McCann

David Wright (Wright)

For nearly two decades, Dr. David McCann has been a practicing Family Physician and Emergency Department doctor. On 9/11, his world changed forever when he responded to the devastation of the terrorist attack on the World Trade Center. Since 2001, Dr. McCann has dedicated his life to the advancement of Disaster Medicine as a fledgling medical specialty. He serves as Chief Medical Officer of Florida OneDisaster Medical Assistance Team and is the current Chair and founding member of the American Board of Disaster Medicine. Dr. McCann is a devoted husband and proud home schooling father of five children.

Dr. McCann welcome to *Getting Things Done: Keys to a Well Balanced Life.*

Dr. McCann, you have a very busy life: a husband and father of five children, a practicing physician, active in Disaster Medicine both in the

US and internationally, a professional speaker and member of the National Speakers' Association. What does living a well-balanced life mean to you?

David McCann (McCann)

Living a well-balanced life leads to a joyful, fulfilling existence in this world. Achieving and maintaining such a balance requires us to set our life priorities properly and always keep them in the right order, even if this requires significant personal sacrifice.

In my life I try to put God first in everything. When I follow His divine Will to the best of my ability, everything works to my advantage and I can look forward to an eternity of beatitude with my Beloved. On the other hand, when I choose to follow my own desires instead, all my plans turn to dust.

After the Lord, I place myself second in priority. This sounds arrogant and selfish, but closer scrutiny reveals the truth—if I do not take care of myself, I will be totally incapable of caring for my family or my patients. Further, taking care of myself necessarily entails maintaining an active prayer life with God so our relationship remains healthy and vibrant.

Third in priority comes my spouse. She and I have become one flesh in the sacrament of Marriage. Therefore, if I truly love myself, I must also love her and make her a priority in my life, as she and I are one. Fourth in priority come my children—the fruits of our marriage. They have been entrusted to us by God to be raised in the fear and love of Him and He will call me to account for their souls at my judgment.

Last in priority comes my job as a physician. Medicine is an avocation, not my primary vocation—marriage is my primary vocation. That is not to say that medicine is not a high calling—it most assuredly is. Nonetheless, medicine is my job, my work, my way of contributing to the building up of God's people on earth. For me to do my work to the best of my ability, I must keep medicine in its proper priority—after God, myself, my wife and my children. Too many physicians I have known in my lifetime have placed their job ahead of their families and often even ahead of their relationship with God. Consequently, they wound up divorced, embittered, and often angry with their patients whom they falsely believed caused their misery.

It is easy for our priorities to get out of balance in our frenetic, depersonalized society. We don't make enough effort to pray. We don't make enough effort to spend time with our spouses and children. I think the key to a well-balanced life is to make a conscious commitment daily not to let that happen and then work hard to prevent it.

It's important to remember that there are four essential elements in every human being. The four essential elements are: 1) the physical part of the person, 2) the intellectual part, 3) the emotional part, and 4) the spiritual part. You have to nourish and work on each of these four elements of the person equally or you won't be well balanced. For instance, in my case I work out physically at the gym one hour four to five times a week with a trainer. Intellectually, I try and exercise my brain by studying toward Master's Degree in Public Health (MPH) through the University of Massachusetts. I am beginning a new job at McMaster University in Hamilton, Ontario in two months where I will be teaching Family Medicine residents and medical students as a full-time professor—certainly a job that will constantly "exercise" my intellect. In addition, I average 150 to 250 hours of continuing medical education per year. I consider life-long learning an absolute must for any practicing physician.

Emotionally, I try to maintain the balance by spending lots of quality time with family and friends. I also spend time meditating on my own. I like to laugh a lot—laughter really is the best medicine! Both social and private time is required to be emotionally balanced.

Last but certainly not least, there is the spiritual realm, which unfortunately for our busy society is often relegated either to the back burner or to no burner at all. Prayer is very important to me. I spend time in prayer several times a day. I try to read the Gospel and the readings of the daily Mass. I talk with God about what is bothering me as well as my hopes and fears, joys and sorrows. I try to thank him frequently both for His many blessings and the crosses He sends me for my own sanctification. I receive the sacraments frequently, especially Confession and Holy Eucharist. The sacraments and the Mass are the center and summit of my life and the source of my strength.

To sum up what I've said, one must work on and develop all four elements of the human being and try to maintain growth equally in each area in order to be a well-balanced person. One must also set priorities in life correctly and work assiduously to keep those priorities in line.

Wright

How do you balance work and family life?

McCann

That's always been my greatest challenge and I will be the first to admit that I don't always get it right. What I've learned over the years works best is to listen to my wife. Women are the guardians of the relationship in marriage. If you listen to them, they will tell you when work is playing too big a role in your life (or if you are not working enough!).

I am speaking to the men in the audience, obviously. If you listen to your wife she will tell you that, "You are not spending enough time with me. You're not spending enough time with the kids." In that way you can prevent yourself from getting too far out in left field.

Men in particular have to watch out and guard against TV/Sports/Internet addiction. These forms of entertainment have their proper place in our lives but imprudent use of any or all of these really impedes quality family time. In fact, it can become a form of idolatry, thus breaking the First Commandment. I have at times allowed the Internet to become an impediment to family life. I was bodily present to the family but plugged into the Net in such a way that my back was to the family and I really wasn't present to them in any meaningful human way. Once I realized I had allowed the computer to overpower me, I made a decision to limit Net time to a bare minimum. In fact, the Internet is disconnected at our home except for specific reasons such as checking email and research.

One of the keys to a happy family life is staying in touch with each other. You should try to have at least one meal together as a family daily—preferably the evening meal so that the parents and children can share the joys, sorrows, difficulties and triumphs of the day. The information so shared then becomes excellent material for family prayer. All families should pray together every night. I firmly subscribe to the old adage: "The family that prays together stays together."

Our family is fortunate because we have been home schooling our kids since Grade 1. We actually have been taking the children to work with us daily. When we built our medical office, we had classrooms built into it with computers, etc. So our children not only have had access to us all day long but they also have seen us in our work roles. In that way they have been growing up with a sense of who they are as people and who they are within the family. They also witness the importance and goodness of work for the building up of the human community.

I should point out that we've been blessed as a family to have a child with cerebral palsy and hydrocephalus as a result of a significant birth injury. We named him John Paul after the late great Pope John Paul II. Our special child really has become the center of our home and has really brought us together as a family more than we ever had been prior to his coming. We thank God for him every day.

Wright

How do you define success?

McCann

My definition of success is somewhat different from what most people would say these days. I define success as this: *"To know, love and serve God while on earth and be happy with Him forever in Heaven"*. I believe if I am successful in living this aphorism, my wife, my children and I will all become saints. Nothing is more important to me than this.

The other measure I have of success is simple--to have two or three real friends before I die. I am talking about two or three people that I can count on through thick and thin, no matter what happens. In fact, I already am blessed and fortunate enough to have such friends so I am indeed a happy, successful man!

Wright

What role does your Catholic faith play in your life?

McCann

It is actually the summit and source of everything that I am. The holy sacrifice of the Mass is the center of everything I do. My family and I depend on the sacraments for the graces we receive from them to feed our souls. They help us to love one another and serve others ever more effectively. The Gospel actually inspired my desire to serve the poor and sick by becoming a physician. It was what led me to New York City after 9/11 to serve in the armory there in the aftermath of the terrorist's bombings on the World Trade Center.

That same desire to serve my country and fellow man led me to join the US National Disaster Medical System. As you mentioned, I am Chief Medical Officer of Florida One Disaster Medical Assistance Team (DMAT) in Fort Walton Beach, Florida. It is one of the nation's premier Level One DMAT teams for disaster management and response.

Over the last several years, my team and I have responded to a variety of disasters including Hurricanes Katrina, Rita and Wilma most recently in 2005 and Hurricanes Charley and Jeanne in 2004. Through out all those disasters, especially Katrina, which was a mind boggling experience, I tried to treat all the victims as my brothers and sisters in Christ. I recall the promise of the Lord that *"if you even give a cup of water to the least of these in my name you will surely not go without your reward."* The gospel drives everything that I do. It also informs my medical practice. What I mean by that is that I'm an Orthodox Catholic so I do not prescribe contraceptives—never have, never will. Of course, I never refer for abortion or euthanasia. I don't do tubal ligations or vasectomies either.

When I was in training, my Orthodox Catholicism got me in trouble a couple of times with my supervisors in medical training. They felt that I should do the things that I didn't agree with morally. Nonetheless, I stuck with my principles, refused to compromise and made it through the program. What is interesting is that in spite of the way our society feels about contraception etc., my refusal to prescribe contraceptives or do any of the other things that are against Catholic teaching has had virtually no ill effects on my practice. In fact, folks where I practice say they may not agree with what I say but they love the fact that I stand for something.

Wright

It is always refreshing to talk to people whose faith plays an active role in their life. I interviewed a close friend of Vince Lombardy, the football coach, and he told me that Coach Lombardy went to church every single day. I was thinking; no wonder all those guys loved the man.

McCann

That's right; he knew how to stay focused and humble.

Wright

Who do you consider your key role models?

McCann

That's easy, first and foremost the Lord Jesus Christ who's perfect God and perfect man, His Blessed Mother, Mary, who is a model of Holiness and humility, St. Joseph, His foster father who is my model of fatherhood and how to be a good worker and then most recently John Paul the Great who taught me to "be not afraid".

Wright

Disaster Medicine is a big part of your life. As Chair of the American Board of Disaster Medicine, you are rolling out the world's first board certification examination for physicians who want to specialize in Disaster Medicine. What do you foresee as the future for this fledgling medical specialty?

McCann

That is a great question. In the last few years' Disaster Medicine has really grown spectacularly and I believe it will continue to grow and become a well-entrenched, well-recognized medical specialty. What it is NOT, however--it is not just a sub-specialty of Emergency Medicine, as some in my profession would have you believe.

My board and I believe that Disaster Medicine is the nexus of multiple medical specialties and asks all doctors of whatever specialty to come together and go back to basics to help communities who have been destroyed to rebuild. Very often in austere conditions--like after Hurricane Katrina—hospital infrastructures were destroyed so there were no CT Scans, no MRI's, no Ultrasound, etc. We doctors are forced to literally go back to using our eyes, ears, nose and touch to make our diagnosis.

We of the American Board of Disaster Medicine do not see a Board Certification Exam as necessary for all doctors who want to volunteer in a disaster. Far be it from us to do that. Any competent, good physician should be able to volunteer in a disaster if he or she wishes. What our Board is doing is creating the Disaster Medicine Specialist who will be called upon to assist hospitals, towns, cities, counties, state and federal governments with their disaster planning and preparation.

Every hospital and community needs a disaster plan. Our physicians who are Board Certified in Disaster Medicine will help these various hospitals and government to develop their plans, test them, break their plans, find the weaknesses that caused their plans to break and then fix the plan.

Our Board is also quite unique. There has always been a dichotomy between civilian academic and military academic medical thinking. The military personnel tended to stay in their group and we civilians stayed in ours. When we called this Board together, however, we made it abundantly clear that the military and the civilians would be equal partners in this venture because who does disasters better than our military?

We now have a significant presence of active forces on our Board and the blending of the academic and military world has been unprecedented and highly effective. We've discovered we can learn from each other and not see each other as adversaries as has been sometimes true in the past.

Wright

With all of the new doctors coming out with all the technology that they have at their fingertips, unlike doctors that I have dwelt with through my life, I'm 68 and that would put the doctors that took care of me a lot older than that. How do they get these diagnostic skills? Are they still teaching them in schools?

McCann

That's a wonderful question. To a degree they are, but nowhere near what's needed. When I trained in Canada back in the 1980s, we had to learn all aspects of bedside diagnosis using the patient history and a good physical examination to come up with a list of potential diagnoses for consideration. Laboratory tests and X-rays were then used to help elucidate which of the possible diagnoses was the correct one. Often, we were certain of a particular diagnosis just based on history and physical examination. These skills are still taught in medical schools today, but honestly the teachers of medicine are relying so much on echocardiograms and cat scans and what not, that we are gradually losing the art of "bedside diagnoses" that was the lynch pin of medicine up until the last twenty-five years or so.

I find a lot of medical residents (trainees) are ill equipped when the power goes off to figure out what's going on in their patients.

Wright

I have a friend who is a doctor; he's retired and about eighty-four years old. Sometimes he suggests things to me and my friends that we tell our doctors. He is such a diagnostician it's unbelievable. Most of the time, if not all the time in my case, he's been right every time without all the expensive machinery. I've gone through the scans and everything because I know that it's best but in the final analysis there is no denying that with primitive techniques he was right on the money.

McCann

Unfortunately that is why our nation has the world's highest percent of gross domestic product tied up in health care. We've become such a litigious society that doctors feel compelled to scan everything two and three times to protect themselves medicolegally.

Twenty or thirty years ago you could have made the diagnosis just by looking at the patient, examining him and maybe doing a few simple tests. How times have changed!

Wright

What is the message that you want people to hear so they can learn from your success?

McCann

The key things for me are: Always put God first in your life. Your family always has to take precedence over your job if you're married. No one every said, over the many deaths I've presided over, they wish they had worked harder. I've heard a number of people say that they wished they would have had another child, and spent more time with their family. So I count success in marriage, in family, and the number of real friends I have when the day is over as the tokens of my success, not how many monetary goods or how many toys I have when the game's over.

The real secret of success is "Run the race until the end and the Crown of Glory will be yours."

Wright

What do you hope to achieve before you retire?

McCann

First and foremost, I would like to get my children through college and help them find their true vocations—whether they are supposed to marry and raise a family, join the priesthood or religious life, or whatever. I hope to get my son, John Paul, to the point where he can walk without assistance. I very much want to spend more time with my wife and family, cherishing them and helping build them up as people—proper to my role as husband and father.

From a professional point-of-view, I would like to see the American Board of Disaster Medicine and its sister organization, the American Academy of Disaster Medicine, growing and flourishing even more than they already are. I want to contribute at the national and international level to improve disaster preparedness and mitigation.

One of the dreams my wife and I have is to open a Hospitality Retreat House for Catholic Priests so that they can be ministered to by married couples and their families.

I am beginning a new job as a full time professor at McMaster University, teaching medical students and residents not just how to be good doctors but to how to balance their lives and promote the culture of life. Perhaps one day I will be Dean of a Faculty of Medicine and able to serve society by improving the caliber (both moral and diagnostic) of future physicians.

Wright

I have an eighteen-year-old daughter, we have already gone through orientation, and in a few weeks she will be going off to the college of her choice. How is the "Home Schooling" going?

McCann

We've been doing it eleven years. My oldest son is sixteen now and he just finished grade 10. Just for the heck of it he wrote the SAT's, even though he hasn't done all the course work required for them. He got double 700's in written and reading and a 580 in math. I thought he did pretty well and that was all from "Home Schooling." All our children do very well academically. The home schooling odyssey is ending this year, however. When we move to Hamilton, Ontario, we are enrolling all five of our children in Catholic school there. We believe they will continue to flourish personally and academically within a good parochial school system.

Wright

That's great! I have often wondered. I've got three children ranging 46 to 18, but they have always been Public Schooled. I've got so many friends that are Home Schooling that I wondered.

McCann

I will tell you how it works best. Obviously, my wife and I are both physicians and even though they have been studying at the office with us, once you get past three kids (and we have five), the older ones teach the younger ones. So you get back to the "Little Red School House" idea. Basically the older ones reinforce their learning because they have to teach the younger ones so everyone ends up learning more.

Wright

Dr. McCann, what a great conversation. I've so much enjoyed talking to you and I've learned a lot. I really appreciate your taking all this time to answer these questions for me.

McCann

It's been a real pleasure. God bless you!

About the Author

DR. DAVID MCCANN is an Assistant Professor of Family Medicine at McMaster University in Hamilton, Ontario. He enjoys teaching medical students and residents while seeing his patients. Prior to accepting the teaching position, Dr. McCann had worked for the last 14 years in a rural area of Southwest Georgia in a traditional Family Practice. He is Chair of the American Board of Disaster Medicine, the world's first physician board of certification for Disaster Medicine. In addition, Dr. McCann is Chief Medical Officer of FL-1 Disaster Medical Assistance Team in Fort Walton Beach, Florida. Dr. McCann is devoted husband and father of five children.

David McCann BSc, MD, CCFP, FAASFP
Department of Family Medicine
McMaster University
Stonechurch Family Health Center
1475 Upper Ottawa Street
Hamilton, Ontario Canada
905-575-1300
mccannd07@gmail.com

Chapter 4

Phil Mandel

David Wright (Wright)

Today we're talking with Phil Mandel, a Master Practitioner of Neuro-Linguistic Programming (NLP), Hypnotherapist, Certified Flight Instructor, long-distance cyclist, accomplished pianist, and recovering engineer with degrees from MIT and Northwestern University. He coaches individuals and leads workshops on topics ranging from Motivation to Getting Things Done to Losing Weight to Reducing Stress.

Phil, welcome to *Getting Things Done: Keys to a Well Balanced Life.*

Phil Mandel (Mandel)

Thank you, David; I'm very excited to be here!

Wright

People often think of success in relationship to material things or accomplishments. What are your thoughts on that?

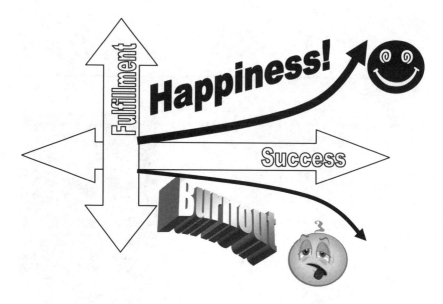

Mandel

Material things trip people up more than anything. Many folks think that if they're driving the right kind of SUV or they've got the right kind of house, they are successful—or that thing is going to bring them happiness.

There's an author you may have heard of—he also does speaking and training—his name is Robert Fritz (www.robertfritz.com). He talks about the success versus fulfillment axis. Some people are wildly successful and have all kinds of money and material trappings, but they don't feel particularly fulfilled. If you imagine a graph with success as the horizontal line and fulfillment as the vertical line (below), these people are over in one quadrant where there is lots of success, but they don't feel terribly good about themselves or their lives (burnout). They're always looking for more. What they think they're looking for is more success, more money, more things, but really what they're looking for is more *fulfillment*, which may or may not go hand-in-hand with material things.

There are studies that show developing countries, for example, where people are as happy as can be. When they are studied by psychologists and anthropologists, they find that these people are having a good old' time even though they work their fingers to the bone every single day and don't even know what a car is! And yet there are folks here in the United States who have won the lottery and come into millions or tens of millions of dollars overnight; if you watch them over time you'll find that many of them are miserable ("Windfall not always a blessing, psychologists say," *The Boston Globe,* July 10, 2004).

Money and material things don't automatically bring fulfillment or happiness. But if we broaden our concept of success to *include* fulfillment and happiness—feeling good about ourselves, being excited to get up in the morning—these are the things that I personally consider *success* and what I strive for myself!

For example, at the moment I have more debt than money. Part of the reason for that is because I invest in real estate occasionally. I either find good tenants who help me pay the mortgage until the property appreciates or I purchase the property and improve it, then resell it for a profit. I'm temporarily in debt because of that, but after I sell something, I pay the debt and put some money in the bank. Right this very minute (September of 2007), I'm upside down—I have more debt than money. I still slept like a baby last night, all the way through the night until it was time to get up, have breakfast, and get ready for this interview. I feel excited about the day, I have a Bridge game later on with some friends that I'm looking forward to, and then I'm going to help someone lose weight this afternoon when he comes over for a consultation.

So, success doesn't necessarily come from having material things or money, but they can help! Sounds like I'm contradicting myself—I'll explain. There's absolutely nothing wrong with having money, collecting accomplishments, and striving for material things. I'm not faulting people for doing this—I do it myself! It's just not the be-all and end-all. It's not that money and material things are by themselves going to make you happy. What I'm saying is that you've got to have more to strive for than just simply "the stuff."

Wright

Speaking of accomplishments, I can see from reading your bio that you have accomplished a thing or two. Since our readers may not know about you except for your bio, would you be willing to share some of the details with us?

Mandel

I'd be happy to! If we take it chronologically, my parents started me on the piano, just like my three siblings. I'm the last of four, and we all started on the piano at the ages of five or six. I had the usual local teachers and played *Clair de Lune* and all the other pieces that kids have to play and then embarrass themselves within recitals.

Eventually, after a move, my parents found another teacher who just happened to be a concert pianist. What a fantastic role model! He saw the talent in me and knew what to do with it. Thankfully, he started teaching me when I was about the age of ten or eleven. That's when my development as a pianist really started. For example, he had me playing all three movements of Rachmaninoff's Second Piano Concerto by heart by the time I was fourteen or fifteen years old. That's a tough piece! Right now I wouldn't be able to play it unless I practiced it for a few months, but back then I had it all right under my fingers. Currently I play piano at weddings, holiday parties, corporate events, and so on; but my pianistic abilities really germinated when the right teacher got hold of me.

I had a great career as an engineer; I have more than twenty years of experience doing electrical engineering work. That also started when I was really young. I used to play with electronics and wires and batteries and transistors as a little kid. I ended up going to the Massachusetts Institute of Technology (MIT) for my undergraduate work, earning a Bachelor of Science in Engineering (1975), then went to Northwestern University for my master's degree (1976). I went to work for various companies and did a lot of contracting over the years. Those degrees and that career have served me well.

I then shifted from working with things to working with people. Doing the kind of NLP coaching I do, it's like *engineering of the mind* instead of engineering of electronic circuits. As an engineer, my life was spent solving problems—"We've got this gizmo we want to build, and right now it's not capable of doing X, but we need it to do X, could you make it do X?" (i.e., run faster, smarter, use less power, do something to stay ahead of the competition). I'd say, "Sure," and go figure out what it took. I'd tweak it and bend it and massage it to get it to do what we wanted. Eventually, we'd get there.

Now I do the same kinds of things with people and their goals. I find out what they want and need in order to be successful. That's where I spend much of my professional life these days.

Wright

You mentioned role models before. I've always heard that if you're walking down the road and you see a turtle sitting on the top of a fence post, you can bet he didn't get up there by himself. I'd be curious to know who your role models were and those you consider to be your mentors.

Mandel

Mentors are the spice of life. We all need them and we all have them. I mentioned my piano teacher earlier—his name was Adam Kapuscinski. When he became my teacher, he saw the talent hidden underneath the *Clair de Lune* and simple Bach pieces I was playing, and he made a mini-concert pianist out of me. His belief in me and his unending nudging to always be better and get the last little nuance out of those Chopin or Debussy or Beethoven pieces, really got me thinking deeply about what it takes to build a meaningful life because everything is important. Every little detail becomes important at some level, especially with music and music is a metaphor for life, as we know. So he was one of my mentors because he had undying belief in my abilities and in me.

I left the New York area and went up to Boston to go to college, and therefore couldn't continue piano lessons with him. Even though he's gone—he passed away in the 1980s—he inspires me to this day! Every time I sit down at the piano and practice something that I learned from him, I see his handwriting on the score and I hear his voice coaching me. He is with me every time I touch the keyboard.

Going back even before Mr. Kapuscinski, I consider that my own father was one of my mentors. He was a very accomplished man. He was a physician—an MD specializing in internal medicine—and very well respected in the community. He was a tremendous doctor and researcher, giving papers all over the world. And he was very, very modest. He never bragged about himself. I remember one time we saw a write-up on him in the local newspaper saying that said he had won some kind of award. When he came home from work I said, "Dad! You won this fabulous award!"

"I did?" he asked.

He didn't even know he'd won it! It just rolled off his back and he said, "Well, that's very nice. What's for dinner?" He was very modest while still being brilliant and accomplished. That was a terrific lesson for me.

Fast-forwarding to today, all of my trainers in NLP have been very influential in my life. NLP turned my life around from a life filled with decades of depression and shyness. I could have never done this interview before the growth that I've experienced through NLP and other means. If I try to name all my trainers, I'm going to miss some and I apologize in advance. People like Tim Hallbom, Suzi Smith, Robert Dilts, and Gerry Schmidt were very helpful to me. Moving on to the one I spend most of my time with today when I go for trainings - Robert McDonald. Robert lives in Yorba Linda in Southern California (his Web site is: www.teloscenter.com). He teaches worldwide. I consider him my friend, trainer, coach, and mentor. The more I think and act like Robert McDonald, the better my life is. And certainly when I'm doing NLP coaching with someone, the more I do what Robert would do and think like Robert would think, the better work I do with my clients. He's been a tremendous influence on my life and has done much to make a man out of me.

It's good to mind your mentors. In fact, I do a speech with that title from time to time for companies and other organizations. I maintain that it's important to thank them when you can (assuming they are still alive). If they're no longer with us, find a way to thank them spiritually, because your mentors play a big part in making you the person you are today.

Wright

You refer to NLP—Neuro-Linguistic Programming—several times. There seem to be many different uses for it and many different opinions about NLP. How would you describe NLP, and how is it helpful?

Mandel

NLP is an interesting field. There are many different opinions about it, as you mentioned. In the beginning, it was over-sold. It was developed in the early 1970s in California by John Grinder and Richard Bandler. They got together and started a field that they didn't know what to name, but they knew they were on to something. NLP is most often described as a *model of excellence*. Let me see if I can explain.

If I want to start a publishing company, I could find someone locally who has published a book or two and find out what he or she did and how the author went about it to see if he or she could make a go of it. Or, I could come down to Tennessee, interview David Wright and say, "David, tell me how to start a publishing company." And naturally, if I go to the best—like you—I'm going to have a better shot at being able to do it successfully myself.

If I want to learn golf, if I would be lucky to get an audience with Tiger Woods—that's what I'd do!

If I want to be a better tennis player and I watch everything Roger Federer does, that would make me better than if I just watch the players at my local tennis club.

Regarding NLP, Bandler and Grinder went and modeled how people think. Not so much what they do, but what's *behind* those actions. What their thought patterns were, what their beliefs were, and how they get themselves to do the things they do, as opposed to just the mechanics. I think of NLP as a model of how the mind works—not the brain, but the *mind*. It's an interesting distinction. You can point to your brain—it's inside the skull. It weighs about two pounds, it's a measurable size, it consists of gray matter and white matter, and it's a certain temperature.

The mind, on the other hand, is harder to point to. It's not limited to the brain. If you're nervous and you feel butterflies in your stomach— well, your brain isn't in your stomach, but there's a piece of your mind that's there, and that's why you feel sensations there. If something else happens and you get a twinge somewhere else, that's because your mind is bigger than your brain. NLP is a model of how the *mind* works. It is very accurate and effective and helps us make deep and significant changes.

For example, I told you that I had been depressed for many years. With the help of NLP, I'm one of the happiest people I know. This is a sea change in this particular individual here because I thought I was going to die depressed. In fact, I thought I was going to kill myself. I had thought about suicide many times, but here I am as happy as can be. A lot of that is because of all the tweaking that I've done with my own mind with the help of NLP. So that's one use of NLP—to make deep personal changes.

Another way to use NLP is to realize, "I'm not quite getting what I want out of my life. I'm pretty happy, but if I could get over this fear of public speaking, I would get up and do more professionally." "If I could get over my anxiety about making cold calls, I would be a better salesperson." "If I could avoid these distractions when I'm in my back swing, I would play better golf." We can help people fine-tune their thoughts, unwind their limiting beliefs, and help them improve almost any aspect of their lives. NLP is good for a lot of things because it's very broad-based.

I invite people to browse the Internet and find out more about it, in particular my Web site: www.positiveintent.net. There's a lot of information there, more than I can say in a short interview like this.

With NLP, one of the things we pay attention to is what we call "meta-outcomes." Meta-outcomes help us get past the limitations we have that are keeping us from getting to the desired results. "Meta" means "about." It's where we get the word "metaphor"—it's something that is *like* something else; it's *about* it without exactly saying what it is—so a "meta-outcome" means it is *about* or *above* or *beyond* the stated outcome.

This is best explained by example. Let's say that I want to have a million dollars in the bank, which is a very common thing that people say to me when I tell them I'm an NLP coach, "Can you help me make a million dollars?" Well, maybe I can and maybe I can't, but the question is this: *What will having a million dollars do for you?* That's a meta-outcome question. In other words, whatever people say they want, if we then have them think, "Well if I had that, what would having that do for me?" then they'd get the next level of outcome, the next deeper or higher goal that they may not have been conscious of until you asked. Back to our example, if you want a million dollars in the bank, great! What would having that do for you?

You might answer, "Oh, I'd finally be able to relax and wouldn't have to struggle as much to make a living." Okay, so what the person really wants is to relax, to not struggle so much. So that's his or her *meta-outcome* of having the million dollars. To be sure, there are other ways to relax and other ways to not struggle, aren't there?

One way to relax in the simplest sense is to sit down and have a nice cup of tea, get a massage, or take a nice hot bath. You don't have to have a million dollars to be able to relax. In developing countries, they don't know what a million dollars is or even what one dollar is, yet they are relaxed and happy and they don't feel like they're struggling. So when we look at the meta-outcome we can say, "What stops you from relaxing now?" These are NLP-type questions, what we call *well formed outcome* questions.

A well-formed outcome comes from asking these questions:
"What do you want?"
"What will having that do for you?"

"What stops you from having it now?" Then you might add,

"What are the first things you need to do in order to get it?"

In order to become relaxed, you don't necessarily need a million dollars. The proof of that is to go out and interview everybody you know, especially the people who seem relaxed, and say, "How much money do you have?" There aren't many who are going to say they have a million bucks! So, the meta-outcome is the *outcome of the outcome*—the deeper level that people are really looking for, behind the surface level that they initially talk about.

Wright

NLP sounds like something that I would be interested in, but I think it received a lot of bad press a few years ago. I thought it was anchoring and manipulation and walking on fire.

Mandel

It's interesting you should say that, David. My introduction to NLP was along those lines, believe it or not. I first heard about it in a real estate networking group. I was at a meeting and I heard all this buzz about NLP. People were saying we should all learn NLP. I started asking them, "Well, what is NLP?"

"Neuro-Linguistic Programming," they would reply.

I said facetiously, "Okay, that tells me a lot—now tell me what Neuro-Linguistic Programming is!"

They said (and this is almost a direct quote), "It's a way to get into peoples' heads and get them to make deals that they otherwise wouldn't make."

I thought to myself, "Okay, this sounds like manipulation, I'm not the least bit interested." I'm a person of integrity, and I only want to behave in ways that are integrity-driven. I have no interest in manipulating anybody. However, there was a little voice in the back of my head that said, "I wonder if that really is NLP or what these particular people are choosing to do with it—in the same sense that you can take a hammer and use it to knock down walls or you can use it to build a house."

I went to the bookstore and found a used book on NLP. The one I happened to pick up was *Frogs into Princes* by Bandler and Grinder, the two co-founders of NLP. I was hooked from the very first page—absolutely hooked! It matches my model of the world, my model of communication, and my model of how we think. It has *nothing* to do with manipulation unless someone chooses to use it as such.

Again, NLP is just a tool—a massive toolbox we can use to do a million different things. If we bring integrity and love with us when we use it, then we are going to use it to help people, not manipulate them.

Wright

What are some of the obstacles you see that get in the way of success?

Mandel

One of the obstacles is our limiting beliefs. If I believe, for example, that I don't deserve to be wealthy or that money is bad or money is the root of all evil (the actual quote is, *"The love of money is the root of all evil"*) it's going to be really, really hard for me to make more than a meager living because every time I get to a place where I might actually get a better salary or a raise or a bonus or a chance to make or acquire more money, I'll find a way to sabotage it because, "I don't want to be like *those* people." Limiting beliefs are probably the biggest obstacles keeping people from being as successful as they want to be. If I feel I don't deserve a good partner in life, if I feel like I'm unlovable, if I have the belief that I'm not worth knowing and loving, then it's going to be very hard for me to find the right person and develop a life-long, close, intimate relationship.

Wright

You mentioned limiting beliefs—it seems like we all have limiting beliefs of one kind or another. How do you recommend overcoming limiting beliefs?

Mandel

Beliefs are interesting creatures. They run our lives in ways that most people are unaware of. I certainly was not aware of them until I had enough NLP training to become familiar with them.

As you might expect, changing a limiting belief starts with *identifying* it. I'm not terribly proud of it, but I had a string of relationships over the years that weren't terribly satisfying. I was frustrated much of the time and I didn't know why. I finally learned through conventional therapy as well as through NLP that I had some beliefs around relationships and around my own self-worth that were stopping me from finding the right partner. I used to feel that any partner is better than no partner. I wasn't happy being single and keeping my eyes and ears open for the right person to partner with.

Also, I had an unconscious belief about money, which was this: "Having too much money is bad." We often look at rich people as though they're different and evil in some way because they have a lot of money. None of this is true. It is just the belief that some of us carry around, as I did.

It wasn't until I changed my beliefs that I became a happier person. Now I can make all the money I want and I can hang out and wait for the right person to come around with whom I can spend the rest of my life.

Overcoming limiting beliefs starts with identifying them. This takes some soul-searching. It could take therapy or counseling or coaching with an NLP practitioner or somebody else. It's important to really find out what's underneath this pattern you want to change. What's keeping you from making money? What's keeping you from having a better relationship? What's keeping you from excelling in your business or your tennis game? What's keeping you from losing weight or stopping smoking? Once people identify their limiting beliefs, then they can seek help in changing them.

Beliefs are interesting to try to change because you can't just say to me, "Oh that's not true, of course you deserve a good partner!" When people used to say that to me, it was like a slap in the face because what

64

they were doing was trying to confront this deeply held belief I had—even though I didn't want to have that belief. It's very, very strange.

Beliefs have to be changed *incrementally*. I would guess that everyone reading this material believed in Santa Claus at one time, and the Easter Bunny and so on. Most likely they don't now, but believe it or not, that change in belief didn't happen overnight. That belief changed gradually. When we became six or seven years old and saw that Mom or Dad was dressed up as Santa Claus, we had this thought, "I'm not sure; *is* there a Santa Claus?" There was *doubt* for a period of time. Then after a while it became possible to believe the opposite. In other words, we started to doubt that there's a Santa Claus, and not only that, we started to believe that these presents actually came from people. Over enough time we realized what the truth is.

So beliefs need to be changed incrementally, and it's easiest to do if you have guidance with it. In my experience, NLP is by far the most effective technology for changing limiting beliefs.

Wright

So how do beliefs fit in other aspects of our lives?

Mandel

Beliefs sit above and organize our thoughts. In other words, if I believe that having money is bad and money is the root of all evil, then that conception will drive my thoughts, which are then going to control my actions. That's how I'm going to keep myself from getting rich. It becomes a self-fulfilling prophecy.

For the purpose of this discussion, I would say that beliefs run our thoughts, and our thoughts run our actions or behaviors. The beliefs become self-fulfilling, and this points to the need to identify limiting beliefs and change them, thereby allowing us to change our thoughts so we can change our actions.

Wright

What kind of personal coaching do you do? And how do you help people overcome their limiting beliefs and become more successful?

Mandel

The coaching I do is based on NLP, and I sometimes do some hypnotherapy as well. I do NLP primarily because it works so well, and I don't have to take the time to put someone into a trance as I do with hypnotherapy. Also, with NLP I get a lot of feedback from the person because he or she is not in a trance. I use the tools of NLP, and I work on identifying limiting beliefs with people, helping them identify their meta-outcomes so that we understand why they want what they say they want, and then I apply the various tools of NLP to help them get what they want.

It's like this (this comes from Robert McDonald my primary trainer): Robert says, "We are like taxi drivers." In other words, if you were to get into my cab, I would flip the lever down, start the meter, and say, "Where do you want to go?" If you said, "I don't want to go to Memphis," where are we going to go? Hardly anywhere! We're sitting there, the meter's running and, as the taxi driver, I still don't know where you want to go. So I say, "Great, we won't go to Memphis. Where *do* you want to go?"

"I don't want to go to Chicago either—I really don't want to go there."

"Okay," I reply, "I promise we won't go to Memphis or Chicago. Where do you want to go?"

As soon as you tell me you want to go to Orlando, we're on our way.

The same kind of thing happens in a coaching session. People come with a medical model that's like going to the doctor and saying, "I feel lousy, I have this pain" or "I'm depressed" or "I don't have any friends," and the doctor is supposed to fix that for them.

What we do is say, "Okay, you're depressed, what do you what instead?"

"I want to be happy," might be the reply.

"Great! If you were happy, what would that do for you?" (That's the meta-outcome question, remember?)

The person might say, "If I were happy, I'd have better relationships, I'd feel more fulfilled, feel better about myself, sleep better at night, get more done during the day."

And then I'd say, "Wonderful! What stops you from having that now?" (A well-formed outcome question, remember?) That's how the discussion starts, and we go from there. We apply the tools of NLP, make a few tweaks and changes, and pretty soon people have what they want.

I try to get things done quickly—I'm a recovering engineer, so I'm used to getting things done, just like the title of this book. That's what I like to do. I like to get things done quickly, get them over with, and help people move on with their lives.

Wright

Any final thoughts to help our readers getting things done?

Mandel

My first recommendation would be to look up NLP and visit my Web site and see more about what we offer and what's possible. I'd also like to suggest that people ask the meta-outcome question themselves. You don't necessarily need a trained therapist or NLP coach to do this. If there's anything that you think you want, like getting a degree or finding a way to get a certain amount of money in the bank—whatever it is, ask yourself, "What would having that do for me? What would I really, really get at the deepest level out of having that?" And when you go deep like that and you find out what is driving you at the deepest level, it becomes much, much easier to get what it is that you want.

Wright

I have heard a lot of people ask some form of that question and they would always say, "What would that *look* like?" This perplexes me because then I would have to make a visual representation, but I've never heard, "What would having that *do* for me?" Now *that* makes sense!

Mandel

In NLP we learn that different people process differently. Specifically, we learn about visual, auditory, and kinesthetic elements, which are the three primary categories that people fit in.

Most people process visually. That's why you hear so many people say, "What would that look like?" Then there's a smaller group of people (which happens to include me) who process primarily auditorially. Remember, I'm a musician—I'm just a pair of ears, and the rest of my body is a life support system for my ears. Then there are people who are mostly kinesthetic. They tend to feel with their bodies and think with their bodies. It takes a little more time for them to process than visuals or auditories. So, if you take an auditory or kinesthetic person and say, "What does that look like?" it's like, "Huh? I don't understand the question!"

Wright

Plus it's such a yuppie-sounding sentence!

Mandel

"What would having that do for you?" is more of a broad-based question. It lets people process in their favorite system regardless of whether it's visual, auditory, or kinesthetic. It's just an open question, and they can process it any way they like.

Wright

This has been a great conversation and I appreciate the time you've taken here in answering all these questions. I have learned a tremendous amount here, and I'm sure our readers will as well.

Mandel

I appreciate the opportunity, David. I'm excited about this *Getting Things Done* project, and happy that you invited me to be a participant!

About the Author

Master Practitioner of Neuro-Linguistic Programming (NLP), Hypnotherapist, Certified Flight Instructor, long-distance cyclist, accomplished pianist, and recovering engineer with degrees from MIT and Northwestern University, Phil Mandel coaches individuals and leads workshops on topics ranging from Motivation to Getting Things Done to Losing Weight to Reducing Stress.

"Phil is sincerely interested in helping others with their goals. He has a unique sense humor and style that makes him stand out and shine. Working with him is always interesting and uplifting and his caring manner makes his 'space' a safe place to be. I give him my highest recommendations and will continue to make referrals to him."—Michael Underhill, DC, Beaverton Oregon.

"Phil's NLP sessions have helped me make better cold calls, improve my level of confidence, and increase my sales."—Kelly Critser, Beaverton Oregon.

Philip H. Mandel
Positive Intent LLC
6135 SW Erickson Avenue
Beaverton, OR 97008
503.887.0889
info@positiveintent.net
www.positiveintent.net

Chapter 5

Jeanne Boschert

David Wright (Wright)

Today we're talking with Jeanne Boschert who has twenty years of solid business experience in management and Leadership development. Jeanne is the founder and CEO of one of the largest privately owned outpatient Behavioral Health Clinics in the Eastern Arkansas Delta. She is also the owner of a commercial real estate development company, and a nationwide consulting and training firm called The HELP Network. She believes that what a person gives in life is reflective of who they truly are. It is this belief that has led to her involvement in The Hope House Board of Directors, the Chamber of Commerce, the American Cancer Society, and the American Heart Association. She also serves on the advisory board for Fidelity National Bank and the governing board for Rivendell Behavioral Hospital. Because of her dedication Jeanne has been selected by the Heritage registry of Who's Who for 2007, as well as being selected as the Small Business Council's Business Woman of the

Year. Jeanne is a Certified Life and Business Coach through LPI and Martha Beck Coaching.

Jeanne, welcome to *Getting Things Done: Keys to a Well Balanced Life!*

Jeanne Boschert (Boschert)

Thank you, David; it's a pleasure to be here.

Wright

What do you feel is the secret to success?

Boschert

It's interesting that there's so much hype right now about "the secret to this" and "the secret to that." People have written books all about secrets to everything from how to be successful to how to be a good parent. But for me the philosophy's really the same, there's really *no secret to any type of success*—that's the secret! Part of the problem is that people are looking for some kind of magic bullet for how to get ahead or how to get above things in life, but I just have to tell you that there's no hidden genie out there. Success is not something that is hiding in the great beyond waiting for someone to find it; it's something that you have to seek and go after with a clear vision and goals you set and work toward.

To me success is not really the answer to what people are seeking in life. When they reach a level the world would recognize as success they realize that it is not enough. There is still something missing for a lot of people and for me it is more important to become *significant*. It is important for everyone to understand that *success is not defined by our career but rather by our character!* It's not that success falls in the lap of some and not in the lap of others—it's a personal commitment and a way of being that says, "I'm going to be the best person I can be today in this life no matter what!"

For me, one of the philosophies is that *success is not defined by what we do, but it's defined by who we are.* As long as I am the very best at whatever it is that I do, and give my very best, then at night when I go to bed I will know that I have succeeded for that day. I just truly believe that this is no secret or mystery. The key is hard work, passion, drive, and commitment. Another key factor is being able to understand what your grounding principles are and what your core beliefs are. Working on these factors is what will take you where you want to go.

Wright

How would you explain your ability to overcome the severe adversities that you have had to face?

Boschert

I don't really actually view them as adversities, I view them more as methods that God used in my life to teach me the principles and the character lessons that I would need for the next phase of my life journey. I'm a huge student of life, and sometimes a very difficult learner, so I sometimes learn things the hard way. I truly believe everything that has come to me is for a greater purpose, and there was a true reason for each experience. I am always humbled by the opportunities that I have to help others in situations through the lessons that I have learned.

God tends to bring people into my life for me to encourage and to assist them in realizing that there is hope, and sometimes circumstances are for our good and growth even though we do not always recognize or accept it. Every defining moment I've ever had in life is probably been in a valley of one of those adversities. I learn more and grow more when it rains on my life. Life has been a huge teacher and I am so very grateful for that. I don't really see the down times as negative impact events, as much as I see them as the foundation for the principles that have built my character and truly made me who I am and continue to build me into the person I strive to become!

I have learned that even though there may be many things that can and will happen, we have two choices we can make regarding them. We can look at the blocks and barriers and the tragedies and we can allow them to create walls around us or we can choose to use those same blocks and barriers to *build* on. For me it was just a matter of accepting the realities of what has happened in my life for what they were and deciding what lessons I choose to take from them.

I make a daily choice to live my life in a building phase. I choose to take the blocks that have been handed to me, and build upon them. My life is constantly under construction!

Wright

How would you advise people to balance their life both personally and professionally?

Boschert

I think that life has more dimensions to it than just personal and professional—there's also spiritual, emotional, physical, mental, and socialized states, and we have to look at maintaining a balance in all of those areas. This book that we are talking about now is key to a well-balanced life, and it all revolves around keeping centered in all of those areas.

When we have a healthy balance in each of those areas, we will be able to remain centered and grounded. So it's more than just personally and professionally—you've got to look at all the different dimensions of your life: spiritually, in your relationships, and social interactions with others, as well as your physical, mental, and emotional areas. It really is all about taking care of yourself first so that you can mentor and take care of others. As we've all heard, when we get on an airplane you are told to apply *your* oxygen mask first before helping those who sit next to you. And that's just the basic premise of life—you've got to take care of yourself before you can be of any benefit to anyone around you.

Wright

What would you consider to be the passion that drives you?

74

Boschert

I could talk forever about passion, but part of the key word here is "drive." Sometimes many people in life let everything drive them, their job, their money, their success, the status—it's constantly drive, drive, drive, drive to the point that sometimes they get driven in places they don't really want to go! It is then that I have seen people look back and say, "How did I get here?" Well, you were *driven* there!

For me life is not about being driven anywhere, it's about being *led* somewhere. And that gives a whole different feeling to how we get where we are going, and it can apply to whatever position we have. I think it is important for people to understand it is human nature to feel that being led down a path is easier than somebody trying to "drive" or push me there.

I see people get into situations where they may become confused and lose site of their priorities. There are times they may even be unaware that this is happening in their lives. I believe they have allowed themselves to be driven by things that are not aligned with their core beliefs and their grounding principles. This leads to a miserable and unhappy person who is bitter with life and cannot tell you why.

I choose not to be driven. I choose to be led with my grounding principles and my core beliefs. You need to know what your priorities are and what's really important to you. For me it is my faith and family and friends. Those are my leading forces.

Wright

What are the differences in people who are successful and can make things happen and those who do not?

Boschert

It all has to do with the motivation. When people are driven by success they're only concerned about adding value to themselves. But when people are driven by something deeper than the need to succeed such as wanting to make an impact on life, then their focus is more of, "How do I add value to other people?"

I want everything that I do to come from the principle that it is going to benefit others or to be measured from the perspective of how this action or project will make life better or easier for someone else. The only way we can truly succeed and make an impact in life is to add value to other people along the way. If that is not our core motivation for all that we do, we have not succeeded; we have failed everyone but most of all ourselves and *God.*

Wright

Where do you see yourself personally and professionally in the future?

Boschert

I hope I am continuing to be a huge student of life, and that I am still learning and seeking to develop in every dimension of my being. My personal growth is vital to me, and I do this by assisting those around me to grow into the best people that they can be as well. I pray that I will always be given the privilege to help others in their journeys of life as well. I tell people all the time that my work is not a job for me it is my mission! I feel that my life is like that of a person who starts out going west—I will never reach the destination. I will always be going west! My life is a seeking path.

Wright

How important do you feel personal growth is to professional success?

Boschert

I think it's everything. If people are not willing to take a look at themselves personally and change some of what they are doing, then they'll continue to get the same results in their life. If you want your life to be more, then *you* have to be more, change will always have to begin with you. It will not be enough to just decide that you want things to change.

I have learned the hard way that *decisions are made with our heads but commitments are made with our hearts!* Personal growth for me is a commitment and it is a huge portion of my mission and purpose. So for me it is not an option.

If a child never learned to walk and never learned to talk, he or she would always be an infant. So for me as a human being, it is more than important—it is *life.* I am not aware of anything on this earth that can live and not be growing and changing along the way. When you think about a plant or anything else, if it stops growing it's dead!

I intend to live life in full expression and continue on the path of personal development and personal growth. I believe that is the lifeblood that will take us to whole new and different levels in our careers. Personal growth is the compass that directs us toward our sense of purpose in life. Without following the path of personal growth we will never be able to find our true purpose and we will continue to wander aimlessly through life.

Wright

How do you view obstacles and what is your advice to those people dealing with them?

Boschert

I would say that an obstacle is not something that is going to stop me. An obstacle is something to challenge me to make the hard decisions— "Okay, this is a key moment, what am I going to do with this now?" Obstacles are learning tools that give you a reason why you can't do it this way again or how you should do things differently the next time. An obstacle has to be looked at as a tool that you have been given to help you break through to a whole new level! You can use it for the cornerstone of building something really, really great.

If we view obstacles and choose to look for the good that can be developed from them, then the possibilities are unlimited. I realize that the majority of the time the pain may be so great that the possibilities to make it a positive get ignored. But if people can only understand the potential on the other side of the pain, and if they can just deal with the discomfort, the discovery will be worth it all!

Wright

Tell me about the "inside-out" theory of life and success?

Boschert

I had a mentor who had shared with me the Acorn Principle. This principle is that everyone is born with an innate blueprint for life just like an acorn. To look at it you'd think the acorn is a funny-looking little seed, and what is it? It's just an acorn. Well, actually there's an oak tree in there waiting to come out! So I use the "inside-out" theory to get people to think about what is inside of them just waiting to come out. We're all born with huge potential and opportunities and desires and passions for what we want in life. Some of the time we just sit on the shelf and do nothing with what we've been given; they become stagnant and may even die inside us.

I talk about living from the inside out and allowing those God-given gifts to come out and to grow. If you grow an acorn into an oak it might provide shade for someone else or it may become a shelter for someone else. I teach others to allow themselves to explore their deepest dreams and desires and to take a good long look at what their innate qualities are that may be buried deep inside. It is in helping others to discover this that I can watch a wonderful life transformation begin. It makes me smile!

Wright

What is important about success to you?

Boschert

It's important to me for people to understand that success is not enough and there's more to life than success. It's about living a life that makes an impact. I know you've heard people saying, "I've got this and I've got that, but I'm still not happy." Part of that is because they've never reached a place of peace and contentment in their lives because success is just not enough. It's more important that people understand that there's got to be a level of contentment within their very soul and within their life at a deeper, more spiritual level. In their relationships they've got to be content and be significant to other people.

There is not a person I can think of, whom I admire as a human being, who has been content with just having all the material things of life. Human beings all have a deep need to belong and to have their soul filled. I have never found a man that has been able to fill his soul with *"stuff."* When people think of success and they are overly driven by that and only that, they never really attain. They keep raising the bar on themselves. They keep thinking, "I've got to get to the next level and then I will feel good about where I am," then they get to the next level and they still don't feel good about their life so they raise the bar again and the cycle continues. What happens is when they come to the end of their life and they still feel as though they haven't attained, the sad truth is they haven't. If a person's goals are internal instead of external then they are attainable for everyone. If a man is looking for peace and contentment in his life, then he is the only person standing in the way of his own success.

About the Author

JEANNE BOSCHERT has earned a reputation as a compelling motivational speaker, an accomplished management consultant, author, and trainer, as well a successful entrepreneur. Jeanne is well versed in a variety of topics and speaks on leadership, empowerment, team building, customer service, managing change, and life planning. As CEO and cofounder of CCI and The HELP Network, she has worked diligently to develop the company into one of the premier outpatient behavioral consultant and training companies in the South.

Jeanne Boschert is a dynamic speaker with a unique style guaranteed to keep audiences engaged, enthused, and energized. Boschert coaches people on balancing their lives, helping others learn to cope in their most difficult situations. She specializes in revitalizing workplaces through teaching her "out-of-the-box" ways of thinking and dealing with personalities. She sprinkles each session with her infectious brand of humor, relying on the everyday trials and tribulations that have made such an impact on her own life and work. Listeners love her, leaving her sessions with a little more spring in their steps and always smiles on their faces!

Jeanne is the founder and CEO of CCI and The Help Network. Through her experience in education, management, and business startup, Jeanne successfully develops programs to meet the needs of today's society. Each presentation is designed to enhance the work styles and lifestyles of the individuals she addresses. Her international travel has offered her a perspective and dimension that has enhanced her passion to assist everyone she meets to live life to the limit!

Jeanne Boschert
The HELP Network
2860 I 55 Service Road
Marion, AR 72364
870.739.5852
jboschert@ccihelp.com
www.ccihelp.com

Chapter 6

Randy & Molly Jones

David Wright (Wright)

Today we're talking with Drs. Randy and Molly Jones, two successful chiropractors from the Monterey Bay Area of California. Together they own and operate the Castroville Chiropractic Clinic, an alternative health and wellness center devoted to helping as many people as possible to regain and maintain their health. They share with us their own success stories of not only career management but also how to keep it all together with a balanced life and have peace of mind. Their warm and friendly healing nature is a refreshing oasis in today's fast paced, stress filled society. You'll find yourself coming back to this chapter more than one time I suspect!

Randy and Molly, welcome to *Getting Things Done: Keys to a Well Balanced Life.*

Randy and Molly Jones

Hi David, it's nice to be with you today.

Wright

Why are you both so passionate about your work?

Randy

My wife and I are both chiropractors and have seen thousands and thousands of people. I think the biggest thing is that we're able to make an impact regarding something that really should be a priority in people's lives—their health. Without our health, we don't have much.

It's exciting to see the changes we can make; not only in people's health lives, but also in their day-to-day lives as we help them get out of survival mode and into more of an optimum health level. The model for the future will be wellness and taking better care of ourselves. Chiropractic really is about optimum health.

Wright

If you had to cite one thing that accounted for your success, what would it be?

Randy

I think it's persistence—just being in practice so many years. Every day there are little challenges that come up, and I think just staying with the day-to-day—just doing the things that need to be done and persisting through them leads to success. There will always be something that comes up to throw us off track. If we can stay on a case with people and if we can encourage them to stay with their care and do the things that they should do to achieve health, we can get the results. I think we can all do that in our own lives in the day-to-day details also.

Wright

What is meant when you say, "I'm not always right" or "give up the blame game"?

Randy and Molly

In the blame game what is meant is that we tend to believe our viewpoint is the right viewpoint. That's not always true, and that equates to judgment. I think any time we judge something it lowers our tone, particularly in a relationship. Tone is the interaction vibes we feel between each other. If you have a relationship with somebody—perhaps an employee or a family member—and you come from a point of view that you're in the right, even though you mean well, often it lowers tone because the other person will feel criticism.

All comparisons are odious; anytime that we compare two people or make judgments, somebody's going to lose. If we can come from the point of view that we're not always right, and we have an open mind on things, I think it can raise the tone and help our relationships. If we are blaming others or anything for our problems, we become victims, and we give away our power. If we can learn to accept others, praise more often, realize we are not always right, and accept responsibility for our own circumstances, we are taking a giant step forward in developing higher self-esteem and a positive ego. The mark of true intelligence is having an open mind on all subjects.

Wright

Let's talk about adversity for a minute. Most people would say, "Let's stay away from adversity," and others say it's really a good thing. I think you and those people who fall there on that side believe that adversity is really a good thing, right?

Randy

I think adversity is a wonderful thing, you just don't want too much of it! At least not at one time. I think a good definition of success is how much stress you can joyfully endure! We all want it to be smooth sailing, and we should be grateful when it is, but think back, when did you experience smooth sailing last? The truth is, as soon as we get one little matter cleaned up, along comes another. The great lesson is to learn to enjoy life in the midst of the challenges.

Adversity is actually a great thing, it really is like what carbon is to steel—if you can take it and call it wonderful. If something comes up and our viewpoint about it is negative or positive, it's human nature to verify our viewpoint on something as being real and we will start to look for evidence to support our belief. Adversity can be a wonderful thing if you see it as such, if you call it wonderful. It causes us to "go for it"—we don't grow during the easy times, we grow during the times when we are overcoming obstacles. I think early on in life there is the development of the soul, so to speak, where we have to go through the mundane, and hopefully later in life we will have gathered enough wisdom that we will not continue to make the same mistakes, and attract the same adversity.

If we look back through history, all great leaders had to overcome great adversity—George Washington, Martin Luther King, even D. D. Palmer, the discoverer of chiropractic—all had to overcome tremendous persecution and ridicule. Even today patients often come in with the wrong idea about what we do, based upon negative beliefs and programming.

Health is a real issue of adversity for people, and symptoms are just a means of causing people to do something about their health. So many people are in denial about their health or situations in their life, and not just their body, but their body of affairs. If they can take adversity and allow it to be the catalyst or the motivator in their lives, they can rise above it.

Wright

My wife is a cancer survivor, and it took about two years out of our lives. She said in a group meeting we attended recently that even though she doesn't want cancer again, she wouldn't give anything for having gone through the experience.

Randy

That's right; life is a continuum of experiences that come our way, and I think if you can have a positive viewpoint (which is about the only thing we have control over—our viewpoint on things), I think we can work through anything. I would never wish adversity upon anyone, especially myself or my family, but as it comes we have to deal with it. The more we attune ourselves to what is right and what is good, the better our world will be.

Wright

Why is it so important to have a clean and orderly environment and to make the most of what you have?

Randy and Molly

I think that environment ultimately becomes an expression of our inner selves. In a cluttered environment an orderly person will immediately go into action and start cleaning that environment up. So our surroundings are a reflection of our inner selves.

The thing is though, often times we neglect things and we become over-stimulated and clutter and disorganization can go the other way—environment can affect our thinking, and so in getting things done and managing our lives, I think it's important to respect the things that we have and take good care of them. If we're driving a junker, treat it like a Rolls Royce and we may end up with one! If we can surround ourselves with beauty, it's more peaceful for us, there are fewer distractions, and it allows us to use our creative intellect. If we are constantly in a stressful situation that's disorganized, it can distract us from our purpose.

Now I know this is difficult to do if you're a parent, let's face it; but eventually you have to be able to change a diaper, eat a sandwich at the same time, and try to be as orderly as you can!

Wright

What are some techniques that you and Molly use to keep yourselves organized and on track with your goals?

Randy

We have worked with many individuals as our mentors and teachers through the years. I think one of the best techniques is to just look at things from a positive standpoint. "Call it wonderful," so to speak ("... and his name shall be called wonderful ..." was mentioned in the Bible in Isaiah 9:6). If we can call it wonderful no matter what comes our way, then again we would start to look for evidence to support our opinion.

I encourage people to give thanks and give praise and have gratitude, so when I get up in the morning I've trained my mind to think, "Lord, I do give thee thanks for the abundance that is mine. This is the day that the Lord hath made, I shall rejoice and be glad in it."

If we can get our minds to start thinking from a deeper level, from a level that expresses and manifests into our lives and program the subconscious, I think that we're going to have a better chance of success; and really, that's the only place success comes from.

Some techniques for doing that would be to create a "dream board." Put pictures of the places you want to go and the things you want to achieve, the relationships you want to have, the kind of career you want to have, and include the various areas of life—career, money, family, social, spiritual, and health. Put a photo of yourself and your family in the middle. Put affirmations of positive things you want to express, put pictures of those things there, and look at it every day. This solidifies these images into your subconscious.

I think positive speech is another really important thing. I once studied with a very enlightened individual who said he felt that health comes from expressions of negativity or positivity and he challenged people to watch their speech. If we see something that is negative, it is best not to give it so much power. I think we all know what positive and negative speech is. We should all look for the brighter side in things, praising people, praising yourself, and praising others. My wife and I do a little game where we will fine each other if we catch the other speaking negatively. She has my permission to fine me twenty dollars if she hears me speaking negatively. She doesn't catch me too often anymore!

Also, one of the techniques that I think is critical for managing our lives is to carry a planner or some kind of system for organization. The conscious mind can only handle so many things, so I carry a planner and my wife carries a planner, and we prioritize our day-to-day lives. I also carry a few three-by-five cards in my pocket, so if my creative intellect gives me an idea, or my subconscious brings forth something, I write it down. This allows the subconscious to communicate with the conscious mind more readily.

Wright

What does "cosmic habit force" mean, and why is self-discipline so vital to success?

Randy

Cosmic habit force is a term that was given to me by one of my mentors, Foster Hibbard, who was a protégée of Napoleon Hill. What that really means is our lives are suspended in our day-to-day activities. We are creatures of habit, and I think it's the survival protective mechanism that nature put into us to allow the species to go on and for self-preservation.

The challenge is that so many times habits can get on the negative side instead of the positive, like exercise, diet, thinking, or speech—the habit of looking for the good in all things and especially people. I think that you can manage your habits; good habits equal a good life and bad habits equal a bad life. That's what cosmic habit force is— you get your habits in order and ultimately they will be an expression of a quieted mind on a level of having a deeper expression of our inner self.

I think it takes self-discipline, and without self-discipline we are at the mercy of our animal nature. All of us have a spiritual and an animal side, and if you feed that animal too much it's going to eventually eat you up! In the Bible Jesus rides into Jerusalem on the donkey. The way this could be interpreted is that He had overcome the animal nature. I think that's what life is really about—the expression of our divine self; but to do that you have to be able to discipline yourself, and not let the animal ride you around!

Wright

Some people find it very difficult to deal with the word "purpose." They search and they just have no idea what they are supposed to be doing, and they jump from one thing to another. Why do you think that purpose is so important?

Randy

I think purpose is paramount in our lives. All of us have programmed into ourselves something that we will be attracted to that we will do. I think that if you have a strong purpose it will drive you and motivate you through times of adversity.

I had a very wonderful nurturing mother, and I think it was programmed into me to be caring about other people. If there was going to be one unique factor in our office, it would be to care about people. Our purpose is to help as many people as we can through chiropractic care and to help them to have better lives.

It is a difficult thing to find one's purpose. I think it takes getting out of the day-to-day routine, I don't think you can find your purpose while you're out struggling to make a living digging ditches. I think you may have to take a day off and go to a quiet area of beauty and pray or contemplate upon it or meditate; my wife and I meditate regularly. In fact, when I first met Molly she regularly meditated and I used to sit around twiddling my thumbs until I decided I would do it too. A mind coming from a quieted state can find its purpose more readily. Both Molly and I practice Transcendental Meditation.

Wright

Do you think there's a subconscious creative intellect, and can it help us achieve our life's desires and keep us well?

Randy

I think there certainly is a subconscious and I believe that there is a creative intellect. I think this inner, innate self is really what is in communication during prayer and it expresses our divine side. That is really where health and healing comes from—that inner model or mold of ourselves. As hard as we think ourselves well, we can't do it—it comes from the autonomic nervous system, which is the physical expression of our innate intelligence.

I really believe that there is a creative side; and I think if we can get in touch with this creative intellect it can hand over inspiring thoughts and ideas. Any one of these divinely inspired ideas could bring us all that we need to achieve our goals—if we will act upon these ideas. And that is the cause of most people's troubles—acting upon the wrong ideas or not acting upon the right ideas or worse, not taking action at all. Action cures fear, and fear is what holds us back.

Fear also causes most of the world's troubles, especially health problems. Most of our health care is fear-based, sickness-centered, disease oriented. My wife and I encourage developing our inner self-image of a healthy body and wellness, and living within the laws of nature. This is what keeps us well.

Wright

How does one break out of a slump?

Randy

In life I think we all tend to slump. For instance, sometimes we may be having a great successful time in our lives, and then we don't discipline ourselves and we get off track, off purpose, and we tend to slump. When that happens there are some things that can be done to break one out of a slump.

Slumps come about because of a lack of discipline, especially with our thinking about negative things. In order to break out of a slump one has to first give up the newspaper (for one week and one week only) and the television. This is because the greatest source of negativity in our lives is the media. Some people who are journalists might not agree with me on this, but this is how it was taught to me by Foster Hibbard. We are programmed by the media; it alters our beliefs and our perceptions and really is a tremendous time-waster. It is depressing, it feeds our negative ego, and it's human nature to be looking for negative things. But the really successful individuals are living their own lives not reliving others'. I would also give up the computer for a week if you are a time-waster or you read the news on line.

Next, read positive books as much as you can and listen to positive tapes and CDs during your commute time. Everybody should have positive books like Napoleon Hill's *Think and Grow Rich* or even this book—*Getting Things Done.*

The next thing is to get to work a half hour earlier. If we can do these things and we can self-discipline our lives, we get a feeling of deservingness—and deservingness is what attracts success. "To Him that hath it shall be given." Have a feeling of deserving and you'll attract success.

Fill every moment of the day with productivity—every chink of time is spent on something that is going to be productive. Do not allow yourself to read the paper at work or waste time. Stay on the highest priority task and you'll get the best result. Go into action; action cures fear and gets results!

Get involved with an exercise program. Exercising causes us to really think that we are putting out some extra effort. We feel even more deserving.

If you will do these things, within a week you will see a turnaround from the slump, and it's all based upon your self-discipline, your deservingness, and your feeling of worthiness. This usually only takes one week, but if you're in a bad slump it might take two weeks—but it always works. Andrew Carnegie taught this to Napoleon Hill and Foster learned it from him.

There's a lot going on in the world about a book called *The Secret,* and what that book is about is "providence moving to"—we attract into our lives what we think about!

Wright

What is meant by "going to the highest priority"?

Randy

If we would focus on our values, if we can find our core values and determine what really is important to us, and we can on a day-to-day level focus on these values and put our energy and our attention and our actions in that direction, then we're ultimately going to have success and have a better balanced life.

Let's go to a higher priority, say for instance, the difference between health and money. If a patient comes to me and says, "I can't afford it," what do you think he is telling his subconscious? And remember, that's where healing comes through. Now, it may be that he can't at the moment afford it, but most of the time what is being said is, "I choose the value of money over my health, I am prioritizing money over my health." What do you think the subconscious is listening to? It's saying, "What did he say? He's saying that money is more valuable than health!" And when that happens often times that same person will go out and buy a new computer the next week because he or she places a higher value or priority on the computer, a material item, than his or her health, which is more of a spiritual nature. If you go to the highest priority, our spiritual nature (that's why we were put on this planet—to develop our souls), and if you can go to a higher level, then a lot of the other things get handled because "providence moves to."

I think if patients were to come to me and invest in their health and put their money in their health, I believe that things would move in that direction and they would have a windfall to help pay for it. On the other hand, I don't think that God is going to support a decision of spending their money at a bar or spending their money on something that is not in their best interest.

If we can go to a higher priority and we can get our values in line, I think it will help us to manage our lives. In the end we will have a much better life and a much better experience here on the planet.

Wright

Molly, tell me why do you think that it is so important for women to work or at least to have their own identity?

Molly

I think as women we owe it to ourselves to watch men. And mostly you will see men working in the workplace. We women tend to have children and stay home with our children, which is wonderful. But what does one do if one has a strong purpose to help others?

I have worked since I've been out of college as a chiropractor. Even as I was having children I decided to continue working for a lot of different reasons. Basically at first I went to work to make money, to take care of the family. Even though I had children and had to hire housekeepers and nannies, that's what I did so that I could continue with my job. Granted, I did go to college for ten years and I got my registered nursing license, and then went on to earn a doctor of chiropractic degree. I didn't want to give that up. I even came up with the clever idea that I could work at home. I opened up an office in my home so a couple of days a week I could be home with the kids, and then I would also go to work at the office the other three days.

Working has given me a lot of latitude as far as being able to express myself and being able to have my own money. I don't really have to look to another person and, granted, even though he's my husband, he's really not my keeper. It has forced me to make my own decisions about my life, set goals for myself, and be accountable for those goals. I have to face myself every day in the mirror and evaluate my life and say, "Listen, this is the kind of life that I have chosen for myself." If there are some changes that need to be made I can take responsibility for those (e.g., working more, accomplishing more, or working less, and spending more time with the family) depending on where I feel there is a need.

The main thing is to keep our sense of purpose and self-worth. Women who earn their own money can have their own say in money matters. Too many husbands use "I earn the money so you do as I say" as a means of controlling and dominating women.

Wright

I don't speak for all men, but speaking for myself, I would rather be married to a happy woman who worked and loved her children, than to be married to a woman who stayed home with the children and didn't love them or didn't take care of them. Ten years is a long time to learn something and then "not do it." I've never been against women working. I think balance is the secret.

How do you keep your personal lives in balance? What are the different areas that need attention?

Molly

When I got married to my husband I had a sense that he and I would still be together after the children were gone. I would joke with him and say, "We love these kids, they mean the world to us, but we need to stay close and keep our priorities so that we're still tight once they're gone. They're going to need us even then—once they've moved on and have kids of their own and we have grandchildren." So I think that's been the thread for me. I've really tried to keep my husband a priority, and keep my personal life and relationship with my husband strong. I've tried to take good care of myself. That's been the priority for me—to be close with Randy.

I know there are different areas in our life, and it's important to keep our lives in balance. We need to be able to rest and have time to recharge our batteries, to pay attention to the spiritual aspect of our lives, invest time in ways that make a difference for ourselves, take time for the children and the grandkids, exercise, and meditate.

Wright

Do you believe that money is good or evil?

Molly

Money is neither good nor evil, only our attitude toward it makes it either good or evil. It is the being/doing and having power of the mind. In our society money is necessary to survive. I think one of the greatest things I've learned is that it doesn't matter how much money you make, what matters is how much money you save. Pay yourself first; this is critical to keeping one's morale up. It is absolutely demoralizing to work a number of years and have nothing to show for it. Everyone can save something. Ten percent is a good number to shoot for; you'll find you can live on the rest just as easily.

In our society money can measure how much we are giving, and how good a life we have. I think money is a wonderful thing. You're able to help people with it. We have a giving account where we tithe regularly, and we give to several places in our community, from the Girl Scouts to the different churches, to the needy families, but most of all we give to spiritual causes we believe in.

Wright

I've always thought that money was great. I had a brother who died early of cancer. When the question is "good or evil," it's easy, but it's easier when it's money or health. He would have given any amount of money to have lived probably one more day!

Molly

We also work to be healthy, we earn that, being healthy is something we can be proud of. We also work to have money in the bank for peace of mind. I guess that's what I meant by that—I didn't mean that being healthy isn't more or less important. I think sometimes people at times won't have enough money and they can get sick. They don't have enough money to feed their families or pay their bills and that can be very stressful. It's interesting to notice just how often money problems and health problems go together. A mind centered in tranquility will manifest abundance and joy, and a side effect will be health and wealth. This is where meditation and our subconscious come in. It only takes one great idea to change our lives.

Wright

Randy, let me ask you one final question. Ultimately, where does success and health come from?

Randy

Success and health come from inside of us. I think success is an "inside job." If we can get our values, ideals, and goals straight in life, and we get ourselves set with a strong purpose, we'll go to a higher priority. Ultimately, that means getting the right things done, which results in a balanced life. If we will work to program the subconscious on a positive level, to look for the *good* in all things, and do all the techniques we've talked about, then our inner nature will express and come forth and we will ultimately have success in our lives!

About the Authors

DR. MOLLY EDWARDS-JONES is a 1981 honors graduate of Palmer College of Chiropractic. She is a doctor of chiropractic, a registered nurse, and a noted colleague in the chiropractic profession. Mother of two and grandmother of three, she is active in Toastmasters and her community. Her hobbies include health and beauty and leading an orderly life. She is extremely popular and sought after for her unique chiropractic techniques and her healing hands.

DR. RANDY JONES is also a 1981 honors graduate of Palmer College of Chiropractic, Iowa, and class salutatorian. He is past president of the California Chiropractic Association MBS, past president of the Rotary Club of Castroville, he holds black belt rank in Japanese Karate, and has produced three noteworthy music CDs of his own compositions. Dr. Jones is a student of all religions and is a long-standing member of AMORC. Using his knowledge of sports injuries, his background in the martial arts, and chiropractic, Dr. Jones has developed a unique approach to help athletes reach their full potential.

Randy and Molly Jones
Castroville Chiropractic Clinic
11282 Merritt St
Castroville, CA 95012
831.633.4067
randyjonesmusic7@aol.com

Chapter 7

JACK CANFIELD

David E. Wright (Wright)

Today we are talking with Jack Canfield. You probably know him as the founder and co-creator of the *New York Times* number one best-selling *Chicken Soup for the Soul* book series. As of 2006 there are sixty-five titles and eighty million copies in print in over thirty-seven languages.

Jack's background includes a BA from Harvard, a master's from the University of Massachusetts, and an Honorary Doctorate from the University of Santa Monica. He has been a high school and university teacher, a workshop facilitator, a psychotherapist, and a leading authority in the area of self-esteem and personal development.

Jack Canfield, welcome to *Getting Things Done: Keys to a Well Balanced Life*.

Jack Canfield (Canfield)

Thank you, David. It's great to be with you.

Wright

I talked with Mark Victor Hansen a few days ago. He gave you full credit for coming up with the idea of the *Chicken Soup* series. Obviously it's made you an internationally known personality. Other than recognition, has the series changed you personally and if so, how?

Canfield

I would say that it has and I think in a couple of ways. Number one, I read stories all day long of people who've overcome what would feel like insurmountable obstacles. For example, we just did a book *Chicken Soup for the Unsinkable Soul.* There's a story in there about a single mother with three daughters. She contracted a disease and she had to have both of her hands and both of her feet amputated. She got prosthetic devices and was able to learn how to use them. She could cook, drive the car, brush her daughters' hair, get a job, etc. I read that and I thought, "God, what would I ever have to complain and whine and moan about?"

At one level it's just given me a great sense of gratitude and appreciation for everything I have and it has made me less irritable about the little things.

I think the other thing that's happened for me personally is my sphere of influence has changed. By that I mean I was asked, for example, a couple of years ago to be the keynote speaker to the Women's Congressional Caucus. The Caucus is a group that includes all women in America who are members of Congress and who are state senators, governors, and lieutenant governors. I asked what they wanted me to talk about—what topic.

"Whatever you think we need to know to be better legislators," was the reply.

I thought, "Wow, they want me to tell them about what laws they should be making and what would make a better culture." Well, that wouldn't have happened if our books hadn't come out and I hadn't become famous. I think I get to play with people at a higher level and have more influence in the world. That's important to me because my life purpose is inspiring and empowering people to live their highest vision so the world works for everybody. I get to do that on a much bigger level than when I was just a high school teacher back in Chicago.

Wright

I think one of the powerful components of that book series is that you can read a positive story in just a few minutes and come back and revisit it. I know my daughter has three of the books and she just reads them interchangeably. Sometimes I go in her bedroom and she'll be crying and reading one of them. Other times she'll be laughing, so they really are "chicken soup for the soul," aren't they?

Canfield

They really are. In fact we have four books in the *Teenage Soul* series now and a new one coming out at the end of this year. I have a son who's eleven and he has a twelve-year-old friend who's a girl. We have a new book called *Chicken Soup for the Teenage Soul and the Tough Stuff.* It's all about dealing with parents' divorces, teachers who don't understand you, boyfriends who drink and drive, and other issues pertinent to that age group. I asked my son's friend, "Why do you like this book?" (It's our most popular book among teens right now.) She said, "You know, whenever I'm feeling down I read it and it makes me cry and I feel better. Some of the stories make me laugh and some of the stories make me feel more responsible for my life. But basically I just feel like I'm not alone."

One of the people I work with recently said that the books are like a support group between the covers of a book—you can read about other peoples' experiences and realize you're not the only one going through something.

Wright

Jack, with our *Getting Things Done* series we're trying to encourage people in our audience to be better, to live better, and be more fulfilled by reading about the experiences of our writers. Is there anyone or anything in your life that has made a difference for you and helped you to become a better person?

Canfield

Yes and we could do ten books just on that. I'm influenced by people all the time. If I were to go way back I'd have to say one of the key influences in my life was Jesse Jackson when he was still a minister in Chicago. I was teaching in an all black high school there and I went to Jesse Jackson's church with a friend one time. What happened for me was that I saw somebody with a vision. (This was before Martin Luther King was killed and Jesse was of the lieutenants in his organization.) I just saw people trying to make the world work better for a certain segment of the population. I was inspired by that kind of visionary belief that it's possible to make change.

Later on, John F. Kennedy was a hero of mine. I was very much inspired by him.

Another is a therapist by the name of Robert Resnick. He was my therapist for two years. He taught me a little formula called $E + R = O$ that stands for Events + Response = Outcome. He said, "If you don't like your outcomes quit blaming the events and start changing your responses." One of his favorite phrases was, "If the grass on the other side of the fence looks greener, start watering your own lawn more."

I think he helped me get off any kind of self-pity I might have had because I had parents who were alcoholics. It would have been very easy to blame them for problems I might have had. They weren't very successful or rich; I was surrounded by people who were and I felt like, "God, what if I'd had parents like they had? I could have been a lot better." He just got me off that whole notion and made me realize the hand you were dealt is the hand you've got to play and take responsibility for who you are and quit complaining and blaming others and get on with your life. That was a turning point for me.

I'd say the last person who really affected me big time was a guy named W. Clement Stone who was a self-made multi-millionaire in Chicago. He taught me that success is not a four-letter word—it's nothing to be ashamed of—and you ought to go for it. He said, "The best thing you can do for the poor is not be one of them." Be a model for what it is to live a successful life. So I learned from him the principles of success and that's what I've been teaching now for more than thirty years.

Wright

He was an entrepreneur in the insurance industry, wasn't he?

Canfield

He was. He had combined insurance. When I worked for him he was worth 600 million dollars and that was before the dot.com millionaires came along in Silicon Valley. He just knew more about success. He was a good friend of Napoleon Hill (author of *Think and Grow Rich)* and he was a fabulous mentor. I really learned a lot from him.

Wright

I miss some of the men I listened to when I was a young salesman coming up and he was one of them. Napoleon Hill was another one as was Dr. Peale. All of their writings made me who I am today. I'm glad I had that opportunity.

Canfield

One speaker whose name you probably will remember, Charlie "Tremendous" Jones, says, "Who we are is a result of the books we read and the people we hang out with." I think that's so true and that's why I tell people, "If you want to have high self-esteem, hang out with people who have high self-esteem. If you want to be more spiritual, hang out with spiritual people." We're always telling our children, "Don't hang out with those kids." The reason we don't want them to is because we know how influential people are with each other. I think we need to give ourselves the same advice. Who are we hanging out with? We can hang out with them in books, cassette tapes, CDs, radio shows, and in person.

Wright

One of my favorites was a fellow named Bill Gove from Florida. I talked with him about three or four years ago. He's retired now. His mind is still as quick as it ever was. I thought he was one of the greatest speakers I had ever heard.

What do you think makes up a great mentor? In other words, are there characteristics that mentors seem to have in common?

Canfield

I think there are two obvious ones. I think mentors have to have the time to do it and the willingness to do it. I also think they need to be people who are doing something you want to do. W. Clement Stone used to tell me, "If you want to be rich, hang out with rich people. Watch what they do, eat what they eat, dress the way they dress. Try it on." He wasn't suggesting that you give up your authentic self, but he was pointing out that rich people probably have habits that you don't have and you should study them.

I always ask salespeople in an organization, "Who are the top two or three in your organization?" I tell them to start taking them out to lunch and dinner and for a drink and finding out what they do. Ask them, "What's your secret?" Nine times out of ten they'll be willing to tell you.

This goes back to what we said earlier about asking. I'll go into corporations and I'll say, "Who are the top ten people?" They'll all tell me and I'll say, "Did you ever ask them what they do different than you?"

"No," they'll reply.

"Why not?"

"Well, they might not want to tell me."

"How do you know? Did you ever ask them? All they can do is say no. You'll be no worse off than you are now."

So I think with mentors you just look at people who seem to be living the life you want to live and achieving the results you want to achieve.

What we say in our book is when that you approach a mentor they're probably busy and successful and so they haven't got a lot of time. Just ask, "Can I talk to you for ten minutes every month?" If I know it's only going to be ten minutes I'll probably say yes. The neat thing is if I like you I'll always give you more than ten minutes, but that ten minutes gets you in the door.

Wright

In the future are there any more Jack Canfield books authored singularly?

Canfield

One of my books includes the formula I mentioned earlier: E + R = O. I just felt I wanted to get that out there because every time I give a speech and I talk about that the whole room gets so quiet that you could hear a pin drop—I can tell people are really getting value. Then I'm going to do a series of books on the principles of success. I've got about 150 of them that I've identified over the years. I have a book down the road I want to do that's called *No More Put-Downs*, which is a book probably aimed mostly at parents, teacher and managers. There's a culture we have now of put-down humor. Whether it's *Married With Children* or *All in the Family*, there's that characteristic of macho put-down humor. There's research now showing how bad it is for kids' self-esteem when the coaches do it so I want to get that message out there as well.

Wright

It's really not that funny, is it?

Canfield

No, we'll laugh it off because we don't want to look like we're a wimp but underneath we're hurt. The research now shows that you're better off breaking a child's bones than you are breaking their spirit. A bone will heal much more quickly than their emotional spirit will.

Wright

I remember recently reading a survey where people listed the top five people who had influenced them. I've tried it on a couple of groups at church and in other places. In my case, and in the survey, approximately three out of the top five are always teachers. I wonder if that's going to be the same in the next decade.

Canfield

I think that's probably because as children we're at our most formative years. We actually spend more time with our teachers than we do with our parents. Research shows that the average parent only interacts verbally with each of their children only about eight and a half minutes a day. Yet at school they're interacting with their teachers for anywhere from six to eight hours depending on how long the school day is, including coaches, chorus directors, etc.

I think that in almost everybody's life there's been that one teacher who loved him or her as a human being—an individual—not just one of the many students the teacher was supposed to fill full of History and English. That teacher believed in you and inspired you.

Les Brown is one of the great motivational speakers in the world. If it hadn't been for one teacher who said, "I think you can do more than be in a special ed. class. I think you're the one," he'd probably still be cutting grass in the median strip of the highways in Florida instead of being a $35,000-a-talk speaker.

Wright

I had a conversation one time with Les. He told me about this wonderful teacher who discovered Les was dyslexic. Everybody else called him dumb and this one lady just took him under her wing and had him tested. His entire life changed because of her interest in him.

Canfield

I'm on the board of advisors of the Dyslexic Awareness Resource Center here in Santa Barbara. The reason is because I taught high school with a lot of kids who were called at-risk—kids who would end up in gangs and so forth. What we found over and over was that about 78 percent of all the kids in the juvenile detention centers in Chicago were kids who had learning disabilities—primarily dyslexia—but there were others as well. They were never diagnosed and they weren't doing well in school so they'd drop out. As soon as a student drops out of school he or she becomes subject to the influence of gangs and other kinds of criminal and drug linked activities. If these kids had been diagnosed earlier we'd get rid of a large amount of the juvenile crime in America because there are a lot of really good programs that can teach dyslexics to read and excel in school.

Wright

My wife is a teacher and she brings home stories that are heartbreaking about parents not being as concerned with their children as they used to be, or at least not as helpful as they used to be. Did you find that to be a problem when you were teaching?

Canfield

It depends on what kind of district you're in. If it's a poor district the parents could be on drugs, alcoholics, and basically just not available. If you're in a really high rent district the parents not available because they're both working, coming home tired, they're jet-setters, or they're working late at the office because they're workaholics. Sometimes it just legitimately takes two paychecks to pay the rent anymore.

I find that the majority of parents care but often they don't know what to do. They don't know how to discipline their children. They don't know how to help them with their homework. They can't pass on skills that they never acquired themselves. Unfortunately, the trend tends to be like a chain letter. The people with the least amount of skills tend to have the most number of children. The other thing is that you get crack babies (infants born addicted to crack cocaine because of the mother's addiction). In Los Angeles one out of every ten babies born is a crack baby.

Wright

That's unbelievable.

Canfield

Yes and another statistic is that by the time 50 percent of the kids are twelve years old they have started experimenting with alcohol. I see a lot of that in the Bible belt. The problem is not the big city, urban designer drugs but alcoholism. Another thing you get, unfortunately, is a lot of let's call it familial violence—kids getting beat up, parents who drink and then explode—child abuse and sexual abuse. You see a lot of that.

Wright

Most people are fascinated by these television shows about being a survivor. What has been the greatest comeback that you have made from adversity in your career or in your life?

Canfield

You know it's funny, I don't think I've had a lot of major failures and setbacks where I had to start over. My life's been on an intentional curve. But I do have a lot of challenges. Mark and I are always setting goals that challenge us. We always say, "The purpose of setting a really big goal is not so that you can achieve it so much, but it's who you become in the process of achieving it." A friend of mine, Jim Rohn, says, "You want to set goals big enough so that in the process of achieving them you become someone worth being."

I think that to be a millionaire is nice but so what? People make the money and then they lose it. People get the big houses and then they burn down, or Silicon Valley goes belly up and all of a sudden they don't have a big house anymore. But who you became in the process of learning how to do that can never be taken away from you. So what we do is constantly put big challenges in front of us.

We have a book called *Chicken Soup for the Teacher's Soul.* (You'll have to make sure to get a copy for your wife.) I was a teacher and a teacher trainer for years. But because of the success of the *Chicken Soup* books I haven't been in the education world that much. I've got to go out and relearn how do I market to that world? I met with a Superintendent of Schools. I met with a guy named Jason Dorsey who's one of the number one consultants in the world in that area. I found out who has the best selling book in that area. I sat down with his wife for a day and talked about her marketing approaches.

I believe that if you face any kind of adversity, whether losing your job, your spouse dies, you get divorced, you're in an accident like Christopher Reeves and become paralyzed, or whatever, you simply do what you have to do. You find out who's already handled the problem and how did they've handled it. Then you get the support you need to get through it by their example. Whether it's a counselor in your church or you go on a retreat or you read the Bible, you do something that gives you the support you need to get to the other end.

You also have to know what the end is that you want to have. Do you want to be remarried? Do you just want to have a job and be a single mom? What is it? If you reach out and ask for support I think you'll get help. People really like to help other people. They're not always available because sometimes they're going through problems also; but there's always someone with a helping hand.

Often I think we let our pride get in the way. We let our stubbornness get in the way. We let our belief in how the world should be interfere and get in our way instead of dealing with how the world is. When we get that out of that way then we can start doing that which we need to do to get where we need to go.

Wright

If you could have a platform and tell our audience something you feel that would help or encourage them, what would you say?

Canfield

I'd say number one is to believe in yourself, believe in your dreams, and trust your feelings. I think too many people are trained wrong when they're little kids. For example, when kids are mad at their daddy they're told, "You're not mad at your Daddy."

They say, "Gee, I thought I was."

Or the kid says, "That's going to hurt," and the doctor says, "No it's not." Then they give you the shot and it hurts. They say, "See that didn't hurt, did it?" When that happened to you as a kid, you started to not trust yourself.

You may have asked your mom, "Are you upset?" and she says, "No," but she really was. So you stop learning to trust your perception.

I tell this story over and over. There are hundreds of people I've met who've come from upper class families where they make big incomes and the dad's a doctor. The kid wants to be a mechanic and work in an auto shop because that's what he loves. The family says, "That's beneath us. You can't do that." So the kid ends up being an anesthesiologist killing three people because he's not paying attention. What he really wants to do is tinker with cars. I tell people you've got to trust your own feelings, your own motivations, what turns you on, what you want to do, what makes you feel good, and quit worrying about what other people say, think, and want for you. Decide what you want for yourself and then do what you need to do to go about getting it. It takes work.

I read a book a week minimum and at the end of the year I've read fifty-two books. We're talking about professional books—books on self-help, finances, psychology, parenting, and so forth. At the end of ten years I've read 520 books. That puts me in the top 1 percent of people knowing important information in this country. But most people are spending their time watching television.

When I went to work for W. Clement Stone, he told me, "I want you to cut out one hour a day of television."

"Okay," I said, "what do I do with it?"

"Read," he said.

He told me what kind of books to read. He said, "At the end of a year you'll have spent 365 hours reading. Divide that by a forty-hour work week and that's nine and a half weeks of education every year."

I thought, "Wow, that's two months." It was like going back to summer school.

As a result of his advice I have close to 8,000 books in my library. The reason I'm involved in this book project instead of someone else is that people like me, Jim Rohn, Les Brown, and you read a lot. We listen to tapes and we go to seminars. That's why we're the people with the information.

I always say that your raise becomes effective when you do. You'll become more effective as you gain more skills, more insight, and more knowledge.

Wright

Jack, I have watched your career for over a decade and your accomplishments are just outstanding. But your humanitarian efforts are really what impress me. I think that you're doing great things not only in California, but also all over the country.

Canfield

It's true. In addition to all of the work we do, we pick one to three charities and we've given away over six million dollars in the last eight years, along with our publisher who matches every penny we give away. We've planted over a million trees in Yosemite National Park. We've bought hundreds of thousands of cataract operations in third world countries. We've contributed to the Red Cross, the Humane Society, and on it goes. It feels like a real blessing to be able to make that kind of a contribution to the world.

Wright

Today we have been talking with Jack Canfield, founder and co-creator of the *Chicken Soup for the Soul* book series. As of 2006, there are sixty-five titles and eighty million copies in print in over thirty-seven languages.

Canfield

The most recent book is *The Success Principles*. In it I share sixty-four principles that other people and I have utilized to achieve great levels of success.

In 2002 we published *Chicken Soup for the Soul of America*. It includes stories that grew out of 9/11 and is a real healing book for our nation. I would encourage readers to get a copy and share it with their families.

Wright

I will stand in line to get one of those. Thank you so much for being with us.

About the Author

JACK CANFIELD is one of America's leading experts on developing self-esteem and peak performance. A dynamic and entertaining speaker, as well as a highly sought-after trainer, he has a wonderful ability to inform and inspire audiences toward developing their own human potential and personal effectiveness.

Jack Canfield is most well known for the Chicken Soup for the Soul series, which he co-authored with Mark Victor Hansen, and for his audio programs about building high self-esteem. Jack is the founder of Self-Esteem Seminars, located in Santa Barbara, California, which trains entrepreneurs, educators, corporate leaders, and employees how to accelerate the achievement of their personal and professional goals. Jack is also the founder of The Foundation for Self Esteem, located in Culver City, California, which provides self-esteem resources and training to social workers, welfare recipients, and human resource professionals.

Jack graduated from Harvard in 1966, received his ME degree at the university of Massachusetts in 1973, and earned an Honorary Doctorate from the University of Santa Monica. He has been a high school and university teacher, a workshop facilitator, a psychotherapist, and a leading authority in the area of self-esteem and personal development.

As a result of his work with prisoners, welfare recipients, and inner-city youth, Jack was appointed by the state legislature to the California Task Force to Promote Self-Esteem and Personal and Social Responsibility. He also served on the board of trustees of the National Council for Self-Esteem.

Jack Canfield
Worldwide Headquarters
The Jack Canfield Companies
P.O. Box 30880
Santa Barbara, CA 93130
805.563.2935
Fax: 805.563.2945
www.jackcanfield.com

Chapter 8

JIM BROWN

David Wright (Wright)

Today we're talking with Jim Brown. He received his MBA from Loyola University in Chicago and his BA from Loras College in Dubuque, Iowa. He has worked in hospital administration and in sales and sales management. Jim has been a motivational speaker since 1991, and has written *A Rose Garden: Living in Concert with Spirit.* He is a certified hypnotist and life coach. His passion centers on his love to work with people one-on-one or speaking to groups.

Jim, welcome to *Getting Things Done, Keys to a Well Balanced Life!*

Jim Brown (Brown)

Thanks, David!

Wright

What do you mean when you say "Life According to Me"?

Brown

I tell audiences all the time, "Every one of us has written a book, and it has the same title. It's *"Life According to Me"*. The problem is, no one has published their book." What I mean when I say, "Life According to Me" is: when you were a child you asked questions. Then you went to school and asked your teachers questions, you asked your parents questions, you asked your grandparents questions—all to find out how life works. As we continued through school we did the same thing. When we started work, we asked, "What about this? What about that?" and we challenged the establishment asking, "Why are you doing it this way?" In all this time we were having experiences and processing this data. Based on those experiences we made conclusions about how life worked in every area of our life.

In my opinion, I think that somewhere between thirty and thirty-five we had enough life experiences to draw the conclusion that I know how life works for me. When we reached that conclusion, each of our books, *"Life According to Me"*, was born.

Wright

What impact does this have on our life?

Brown

Once we draw conclusions about how life works, life can't do anything other than give us what we've decided we deserve. **The key is: what do I believe I deserve from life?** If I don't believe I deserve something, I'm not going to get it; I'll keep pushing it away.

For example, our son called me one day asking how he should handle a problem he was having with the woman he was having a relationship with. I asked him, "At what point in a relationship do you start to sabotage it?"

"In two months, Dad," he answered.

What happened in his case was because of his fear of intimacy, as they got closer, suddenly something inside was triggered telling him,

"Whoa! Let me put the breaks on! I don't want to get any closer! Get me out of this relationship!" At some point he had been hurt and. when we get hurt, what do we do? We go inside ourselves and we retreat because that pain is so great we don't know how to deal with it. Because we don't want to be exposed to that kind of experience again, we sabotage the relationship before we get close enough to experience that level of pain rather than take the risk of loving again.

Look at the people in life we consider great successes. Let's use Walt Disney as an example. How many times did he go through bankruptcy? Or consider Jack Canfield and Mark Victor Hansen. How many publishers told them, "You guys can never sell short stories. Nobody will ever buy them." But they have sold over 85,000,000 *Chicken Soup for the Soul* books! What they did different was they didn't let the pain stop them—they moved through it. They didn't allow it to define them, and I think that's the key. We have to move through the pain because all of us are going to have "failures" in life. That's the way we learn and grow.

Wright

Do you think people are aware that they're doing this?

Brown

Absolutely not, I think that life is lived on several levels. Some people live life as if it's a game of Monopoly. They live as if the purpose of life is to accumulate cars, houses, boats, money, and vacations, and the guy who dies with the most things wins the game of life. I believe that there's a deeper meaning to life, but if we're living life on the surface—on the materialistic level—we're saying, "It's all about accumulating material wealth." If we don't accumulate it then we consider ourselves a failure.

What if we were to see our life as a journey that has nothing to do with the destination? What if we were to stop and ask, "Who am I becoming in the process of moving through all these experiences that some people think are "tragedies"? Then we would look at our negative experiences as opportunities for us to learn and grow. When I perceive an experience as an opportunity I'm going to ask myself more effective questions. For example, I may ask myself what the situation is trying to teach me or how else I can look at it, or what I have to believe about this in order for me to change the way I feel about the experience.

For many years I would close a lot of my programs by asking, "Have you heard of *Footprints?*" Some call it a prayer; some call it a poem. I would act it out as a two-person play, and I would never look at the audience. It is a story about a man having a dream. In his dream he was walking along a beach with God, and he looked up and saw all the scenes in his life. He saw two sets of footprints in every scene, and then he looked over there in the last scene of his life and saw only one set of footprints. He noticed it was really hard at the end of his life, and he looked back and he saw a whole bunch of places where there was only one set of footprints and noticed that each time he only saw one set of footprints it was at a particularly "difficult" time of his life. He said, "God, you promised me that if I found You that You would take care of me, and here I am in the hardest times of my life and there's only one set of footprints. What did you do—did You abandon me?"

And then I'd turn and face the person who was talking, as if I were God, and I'd hold that person's face in my hands and I'd say, "Honey, when you only saw one set of footprints that's when I was carrying you. I'd never abandon you."

I would then stop and turn to the audience, and say, "I invite you to close your eyes, climb up on God's back, wrap your arms around His chest, and your legs around His waist, and let Him carry you through!" (I invite you to do this right now)

Wright

Are you saying that we have to become consciously aware of how our thoughts and our beliefs are affecting our life?

Brown

If we are not aware of our thoughts and our beliefs and how they are affecting our life, then we will not see any conscious connection between our thoughts, our beliefs, and the events in our life.

The mentality that we have in the society we live in is that we're victims. If I believe I'm a victim, there is nothing I can do to avoid any particular situation. What do I do if I'm a victim? I blame, and when I blame I don't accept responsibility for creating the experience. In order to change this, I need to be aware of how I'm thinking, and to accept that thoughts create.

There are many books written about that, and in my book *A Rose Garden, Living in Concert with Spirit,* I write that we think about 60,000 thoughts a day—the problem is that 99 percent of them are the same thoughts we thought yesterday. Monitoring our thoughts is very difficult. In her book, *The Law of Attraction,* Esther Hicks wrote about this in terms of monitoring our emotions. Emotion-wise I know two things: either this feels good or it doesn't. That's easier to monitor. If it doesn't feel good, what thought do I need to have to feel better?

We are constantly having thoughts. When we repeat the thoughts consistently, they become beliefs. For example, let's say that your father abused you as a child and you developed a belief about how to deal with him to get through this trying time in your life. Now you are grown up and on your own, but you still have this belief about how men behave and it is preventing you from having a meaningful relationship with a man. One thing to do is realize that this belief enabled you to get through the period when you were being abused. Therefore, it served you to believe that men are abusive. Then ask yourself, "Now, does this belief still serve me?" If the answer is no, then get rid of that belief and replace it with a belief that serves you today on the path you now want to travel.

Wright

What do we do once we are aware of how our thoughts and beliefs affect our life?

Brown

First decide which beliefs still serve you. Keep those beliefs. The next thing to do is to accept that you create your life by the thoughts you consistently have. If you *don't* accept that you create your life, the only other option is that you are a victim. If you believe you're a victim then don't read any further. (Now, this is my opinion. Realize that all we're talking about here today, is from my point of view.)

If an aspect of your life isn't working for you, be open. You might be thinking, "What he's saying makes sense to me. I buy the idea that we create our life by our thoughts, but I didn't know I did that; therefore, I don't want to admit it because when I look at my life it's in shambles." It's like looking down at a pile of manure and not wanting to admit that you created that pile of manure. But that's not the issue, David; the issue isn't whether my life is a mess or that I created it—it's that I wasn't aware that I could create! Now that I know I can create, what am I going to do with that newfound power? I'm not going to create manure anymore! I want to create gold, now that I know I can do it. That's the key—let go of what the past was because I can't do anything about it anyhow. It only exists as a perception in my mind.

We have to completely reject the concept that we are a victim because thinking this way will *never* serve us.

Wright

Are you saying that we are 100 percent responsible for our life and there are no victims?

Brown

Yes. If I believe I am a victim, it means I can do nothing to change it. When I believe I'm a victim I get angry, I get resentful, I get hostile; I want revenge and I want to blame people.

I teach a class in mind/body/spirit connection. I start the class by saying, "Let's assume that before you come down into this life, you designed the life that you wanted in order to learn the lessons that you need to learn. You pick your mom and dad, you pick your sex, your color, the country where you're born—all the rest of the circumstances of your life. People are going to *agree* to play a certain role in your life. It will be as though you're in a play—all the people in your life are going to play their certain role because they love you so much and they are willing to play even the role of a villain to help you learn your lesson."

As an example of this, I had a spiritual teacher I admired immensely. I said to my wife, "We want to start investing in income property. Why don't we offer to let her find a house? We'll buy it, and then all she'll have to do is pay the rent." She found the house she wanted to live in for the rest of her life and we bought it. Three and a half months later she hadn't paid us any rent. Because this was somebody I loved and admired I hadn't done a credit check. I didn't have her social security number and I didn't have background information on her. I had to evict her, take her to court and sue her. I got my money back but what I learned was to not give my power away. Instead of feeling that I had been victimized and that she had taken unfair advantage of me, I learned a valuable lesson. Initially I had thought, "Whoa, she has these spiritual gifts. She's better than I am; how wonderful! Why don't we buy her a house and maybe she'll think more highly of me." In doing that I was giving my power away.

When I took my power back I took the action I needed to protect our investment and I sent her love every day until I could think about her without any emotional attachment.

When we play the role of a victim, we give our power away. Playing the role of a victim isn't going to change the circumstance. If you decide you are going to accept responsibility, then you are saying, "What am I trying to *learn* from this?"

Another example is about a man who fell while rock climbing. He landed on his neck causing serious damage. The doctors performed surgery and were able to give him upper body mobility. He now looks back at that situation and says, "Had that not happened, I would have been dead a long time ago because at that time I was on drugs." He would not have gone rock climbing that day had he known he was going to have such a serious accident, but the accident was an incredible lesson that he learned and it may have even saved his life.

Wright

Let's go back. You don't believe that there's any circumstance where people are victims. What about a random shooting or a hurricane or a tsunami or children with a terminal disease—aren't those people victims?

Brown

I'm sitting in my library and I've got seven hundred books here, most of them are about God, life, growth, and about how all of these kinds of circumstances impact our life. My belief is that we came here and we're alive in order for our soul to grow. We came to this "earth school" and we chose these lessons—we created these circumstances so that we could learn by coming to school.

You mentioned that you sent your daughter to the university. She's going to the university and she has decided to major in a certain subject. Each one of us decides to major in a certain subject in life. According to Sylvia Browne, we have seven option lines to choose from: family, social life, love, health, spirituality, finance, and career.

What if God says, "I need somebody to volunteer to live for eighteen months? If you volunteer, you will be born with a hole in your heart and you'll die in a year and a half, but because of that you're going to teach your mom and dad how important love is in life."

In November of 2001, I gave a talk on a cruise ship that I titled "The Gifts from September 11." The way I opened was to say, "Imagine that you were in this incredible ballroom before you came down to earth. In walked your Creator and your Creator says, 'I need 3,000 of you to volunteer to be born in different places on Earth. You're going to come together from all the different countries of the world on September 11, 2001, and you're all going to die. However, because of the way you are going to die, the entire world is going to rethink how important love is, how important it is to be compassionate, how important it is to be tolerant and accept people of different colors or religions or beliefs and you're going to help them.' " Then I asked the audience, "How many of you would volunteer to have your life stand for that?"

In answer to your question, no, I don't believe that there are any circumstances in which we are a victim!

Wright

Are you saying that we are the co-creator of our life?

Brown

Yes, we co-create our life by our thoughts and beliefs. I think we are just the physical extension of our Creator. He has given us all of His powers and we haven't accepted that we deserve to live at such a high level. I think that we go around believing we're all midgets, when in reality we're all giants.

There's a story about a bunch of chickens in a hen yard, and there was one eagle. He was born there with the chickens, so all he knew were the chickens and he acted like a chicken. One day they saw another eagle soaring overhead. They all said, "Ah, if I could only fly like an eagle!" In this hen yard was an eagle that could do everything that the eagle soaring above could do but because he thought he was a chicken he never even attempted any of the feats he was witnessing.

To me we're all eagles/giants and we don't know it. We need to be able to support each other and say, "Hey, you're incredible! Step up here—become all that you can be."

That's what I admire about Jack Canfield and the work he does. I get his newsletter once a week. His newsletters are geared to empowering people.

I received an e-mail recently that said, "If you don't think that you make a difference, just try going to sleep at night with a fly in your bedroom. If a little bitty fly makes that kind of difference, we need to understand that we make a difference too.

In the first *Chicken Soup for the Soul* book there was a story about a high school senior teacher in California who brought each student in front of the class and told them how they made a difference. Then she presented each of them with a blue ribbon imprinted with gold letters which read, "Who I Am Makes a Difference". She gave each one of them three more ribbons and told them to go out into the community and spread this acknowledgment ceremony. One boy went to a junior executive in a nearby company who helped him plan his career. He gave him two extra blue ribbons and asked him to find somebody to honor. This man gave one to his boss and told his boss to honor somebody else with the last ribbon. His boss went home to honor his 14-year-old son. He told him that he makes a difference to him and beside the boy's mother the boy was the most important person in his life. "You're a great kid and I love you!"

The startled boy started to sob and sob, and he couldn't stop crying. He looked at his father and said through his tears, "I was planning on committing suicide tomorrow, Dad, because I didn't think you loved me. Now I don't have to."

Little things like this that we have no idea about can make an impact on somebody else.

Wright

How do we do this?

Brown

The first thing to do is to decide which area of our life we want to change the most. When I undertake a project I look at it two ways: The first way is to ask myself, "Do I want to tackle the hardest thing first to show that I can conquer the biggest thing and then everything else is easy?" The other way—the way I usually take it is, "What is something that I believe is the easiest thing to change?"

Take an area of your life that you would like to change, whether it's your personal relationships, financial situation, a work situation, your spiritual life—what do you want it to be?

Write a detailed description of *how* you want it to be. When most of us attempt this task we will temper our wish list by saying, "Well I don't know how that could happen, so I'm not going to put that down because I don't have any life experience that's going to tell me I can make that happen." We have to surrender control.

I'll use the example of Santa Claus. When we were kids and Mom would ask, "What do you want for Christmas?" and we would just make a list of what we wanted, and give it to her. We never questioned if she and Dad had the money, or if what we wanted cost too much or how they would get it. We just accepted that we made a list out and we gave it over to be fulfilled. The beauty in that simplicity is to understand it is *not* your responsibility to figure out "how" to make it happen.

Once you have written how you want your life to be, which is your updated version of *"Life According to Me"*, then get as many pictures as you can that would represent how you want your life to be in that particular area you've chosen. Spend ten to fifteen minutes a day either looking at those pictures or meditating or dreaming about how you want your life to be. When you do that, forget about *how* it's going to happen—your only job is to get the feeling. You're engendering the feeling of what it would be like if you owned a beach home or if you were president of the company—what would having the beach house or being the CEO feel like?

You are making use of the Law of Attraction to create your life the way you want it to be. It's similar to going into a restaurant and ordering the food you want to eat. You place your order and continue your conversation assuming you are going to get what you ordered.

You can do that same thing with every area of your life. All you have to do is to believe that you deserve it and to trust that it's going to come.

Wright

What problems do we create by having our unpublished version of *Life According to Me?*

Brown

Effectively, what we have done is argue for our limitations. If we argue for our limitations, they are ours! Doing this makes it difficult to have successful relationships. For example, over 50 percent of first marriages fail, and 75 percent of second marriages fail. My point of view is that a big reason a higher percent of second marriages fail is because the divorced party blames his or her spouse, "It's all her [or his] fault that we got divorced." When people blame, they don't accept responsibility for creating the experience and don't make the necessary changes in their life. Consequently, they go out and find the same kind of person they divorced the first time only to end up with the same result.

Instead, take inventory and say, "How did I create this? What do I need to *do* differently, how do I need to *think* differently, how do I need to *believe* differently in order to make my life successful?"

My wife and I just celebrated our fortieth anniversary. We're at a place where I can't even imagine life without my wife. And I don't have to *do* anything, just sit in the same room with her to *be* there with her. I look at her and I think about how blessed and how lucky I am to have her as my wife.

When I see a couple who are engaged or I go to a wedding, I'll tell the couple, "I have one exercise for you that will guarantee you'll have a happy marriage. Take about thirty seconds a day for the rest of your life and say to your spouse, 'What I love about you is—' " What this does is it causes them to *look* for what they love about each other.

As a husband you shouldn't say, "Well, honey, what I love about you is that you are a great housekeeper," and then say that every day for a week or a month. When you start looking for the many reasons why you love her you will always find what you are looking for.

If you're a manager, look for the good things people do, and if you catch people doing things right, reward them. Keep pom-poms in your bottom drawer and every time they do something right take those pom-poms out and tell them how incredible they are; then, they are going to live up to that expectation.

Wright

What is the most important thing you want our readers to remember?

Brown

First, no matter what is going on in your life, that life is just absolutely awesome! People need to be able to forget about the past. The past was there in order to teach us, just like when we were in grade school and we had to learn the multiplication tables. We didn't get to go to the three times table until we learned the two times table. Once we learned that lesson we went on to the next lesson. It is my belief that we came to Earth school to learn lessons so we can grow our soul. Embrace all of life's lessons as blessings that give us the opportunity to grow spiritually.

Life is awesome; we're going to forget about our past, and we're going to dream about the future that we want to create. And when we're dreaming, we're going to surrender the need to figure out how it's going to happen. Lastly, I need to believe in myself and absolutely know that I deserve the best life has to offer. And then I simply release my whole life into the hands of my Creator.

Wright

What a great conversation. I really appreciate the time you've taken with me to answer all these questions.

Brown

You're welcome. It was a lot of fun!

About the Author

JIM BROWN earned his MBA from Loyola University in Chicago and his BA from Loras College in Dubuque, Iowa. He has worked in hospital administration and in sales and sales management. He has been a motivational speaker since 1991. Jim is author of *A Rose Garden: Living in Concert with Spirit,* and he is co-author with Jack Canfield in the book, *Getting Things Done: Keys to a Successful Life.* He is a life coach and certified hypnotist.

His passion centers on his love of working with people one-on-one or in a group to make a difference in their life.

Jim Brown, MBA
Brown and Associates
8432 Denise Lane
West Hills, CA 91304
800.995.1426
jim@jimbrownspeaker.com
www.jimbrownspeaker.com

Chapter 9

CYNTHIA SHELBY-LANE, MD

David Wright (Wright)

Today we are talking to Cynthia Shelby-Lane, MD, also known as the *Ageless Doctor*. She is a graduate of the University of Michigan Medical School and Second City Comedy School in Chicago. She trained as a surgeon at the University of Texas in Houston, Texas. She practiced Emergency Medicine for over twenty-three years. As an Emergency Physician she handled life-threatening emergencies at Detroit Receiving Hospital, a Level I Trauma Center in Detroit, Michigan, and she was the director of Emergency Medicine at Hutzel Hospital for ten years.

Her experiences in dealing with life and death crises in the emergency room allowed her to see and realize the benefits of medical technology and the limitations of traditional medicine. This led her to seek methods of prevention, holistic, and integrative medicine, which is now known as anti-aging and regenerative medicine, before these methods were even popular.

She has been board certified in anti-aging and regenerative medicine since 1997. She is also an Oral Board Examiner for the American Academy of Anti-Aging Medicine and has completed her fellowship and Master's Program in Anti-Aging Medicine & Regenerative Medicine.

Her thesis is titled "Laughter Is Good Medicine." The foundation for the research of this program will be based on current university studies, programs at cancer hospitals and cancer organizations, and interviews with top comedians and humorists.

Cynthia, welcome to *Getting Things Done: Keys to a Well Balanced Life.*

Cynthia Shelby-Lane (Shelby-Lane)

Thank you so much, David.

Wright

You are known to many as the "Ageless Doctor." How did you get that title and what does it mean?

Shelby-Lane

Ageless Doctor is a title that is probably as self-appointed as much as it has been earned. As you stated, I graduated from a traditional allopathic, medical school and practiced front-line medicine with gun shot wounds, vehicular trauma, heart attacks, infections, and accidents and injuries for at least twenty-three years. The unexpected was always "the expected." When you practice medicine in an emergency room setting, you realize that you are doing a vital service for the sick and injured in our country and worldwide, especially when that person has nowhere else to go for healthcare, 365/24/7. This, of course, means the insured as well as the uninsured because heart attacks and injuries happen to everyone. No one is spared the illnesses and trauma of everyday life and living.

When you finish medical school you take the Hippocratic Oath, *Do No further harm . . .* and somehow you create your own meek persona and you decide what kind of doctor it is you really want to be. I became an MD, which is basically twenty-five years as a "Medical Detective." I worked as an ER doc, and was known as today's version of "House," solving people's illnesses, trying to discover the cause or the reason they presented to the Emergency Department (especially when it wasn't obvious), deciding who should stay and who should go home, and, of course, pronouncing many people dead—including infants, children, and adults—very heartbreaking work. With all of that heavy-duty work, "prevention" was the only thought that prevailed, day in and day out. My desire and passion for health, prevention and quality of life became a daily mantra and therefore, the term "Ageless Doctor." I then started practicing on myself, my family, and my friends, taking supplements, exercising, eating more healthy, avoiding soda pop—everything but stress reduction. (I am currently using holosync meditation and hypnosis tapes that have made a huge difference in my stress response.)

Wright

You were trained as a surgeon and practiced emergency medicine for over twenty-three years. What happened to cause you to change your practice to alternative and prevention medicine?

Shelby-Lane

I was a little dismayed by seeing and treating so many sick and injured people and it was very difficult to see and treat people who were very sick, in lots of pain, injured and dying on a daily basis. I also had no time for myself and family. Very few thanks for a job well done. I literally did this for over two decades. I then began to really wonder what makes all this illness happen repeatedly, without fail, and was the only remedy drug therapy, surgery, and heroic resuscitation? How then can chronic illness be prevented, even reversed? I completely shifted my thinking in terms of who is doing this *"fountain of youth"* medicine? People have been looking for the *fountain of youth* since Cleopatra's time. So, that was my next venture—to find out, not so much how to stay young, but how to stay young and healthy.

That's when I attended a medical conference titled, "Physician Heal Thyself," where I met an incredible cardiologist, Dr. Robert Eliot, author of the book, *From Stress to Strength, How to Lighten Your Load and Save Your Life.* I did poorly on his self-help quiz that was offered during his session. After his lecture, I went to the front of the meeting room and introduced myself, looking for guidance. I told him that I was an emergency physician working midnights and I loved it. He almost fell off of the stage. He was already seated, but he leaned back abruptly and warned me to "get out" while I was still alive. I'll never forget the look on his face. He scared me. I wasn't even aware that all the good work I was doing was really killing me. He also told the story of how his heart attack, at the age of forty-four, saved his life. Self-diagnosed, while at work, he admitted himself into the CCU and from that day forward, made changes to stay alive and stress free.

After that conference, even more thoughts ran through my mind every day while working the dreaded midnight shift, and the questions were, "How can I do something about this? What else can I do?" I thought about my years of training; my life being cut short due to work stress— stress that I loved and had become accustomed to. I wondered how I could change my life and make the transition. I was frequently stopped by my staff. After babbling on and on about prevention, they would tell me "this is the emergency room. If you want to do something else, you should go on about your business, but right now we have two gun shot wounds, a heart attack, and a hang nail, so get back to business"—the business of saving lives and patching people up, but, not the business of prevention and healing.

Every morning (or evening) when I got up to go to work, I thought, "There has to be something else. There has to be something about serious prevention in healthcare—prevention versus cure. It's not very sexy. There's no money in preventing illness. But, it's very important. An ounce of prevention…" You've heard it over and over.

When I entered medical school, I had thought there should be more emphasis on how to stay healthy as opposed to how to fix illness. Prevention was not a focus in medical school. The focus was on the other

"P" words: physiology, pathology, and pharmacology. That's still true today, but it's slowly changing. The public is demanding help to the tune of fifty billion dollars in sales per year in out of pocket expenses for co-pays and preventative healing methods. They want health and vitality, not drugs. But they need educated assistance with the process—not more information per se, but *recommendations* from someone who is qualified.

I knew that emergency medicine was solid and necessary medicine, but I also knew enough about alternative therapies from the literature to pursue what had become my passion. I was destined to be involved in the search and practice of "the fountain of youth medicine." Even when I entered the field of Emergency Medicine it was a brand new specialty, now servicing over one hundred million people per year nationwide, and even more worldwide. Since then other concerns have come along, such as Baby Boomers who want to stay young and vibrant. That is when I found the American Academy of Anti-Aging Medicine. I started going to conferences and took my board exam to become board certified. Since then I have completed the fellowship in anti-aging and regenerative medicine.

Getting things done in medicine is like anything else in life. It involves hard work, smart thinking team players, and mentors near and far, and asking the right questions. That includes patients and the healthcare providers. My medical mentors have progressively shaped my thinking and I have quite a bit to be thankful for.

I had the experience and privilege of working with the best teachers and leaders in the field of Emergency Medicine at Wayne State University. They are known worldwide as the grandfather and grandmother of Emergency Medicine, Drs. Krome and Tintinalli. The field of emergency medicine has also been influenced by an ER doctor in Detroit, Dr. Manny Rivers. I have never worked with him but I truly admire his work in resuscitation. He is an incredible doctor/researcher. These kinds of doctors have shaped the profession and the practice of Emergency Medicine in Detroit and worldwide because of their dedication to the profession.

But as time went by, I started looking outside the box and found other folks who have become my anti-aging mentors, doctors like Drs. Klatz and Goldman, who founded the American Academy of Anti-Aging Medicine, and Dr. Pamela Smith, who also practiced emergency medicine with me. We both went on the trail to forge a new path for people staying young. Dr. Pamela Smith, as the founder of the fellowship for Anti-Aging and Regenerative Medicine, has been quite a leader in the anti-aging field worldwide with the fellowship program. There are others such as Drs. Stephen Sinatra and James Roberts, both cardiologists, and Dr. Mark Houston, a hypertension specialist, who have done incredible work in the field of heart disease and prevention. I am also working with the American Heart Association, to help educate the community about heart disease and stroke prevention. My friend and colleague, Dr. Maria Sulindro is also in this group of forward thinkers and there are many, many others. These are just a few of the incredible doctors worldwide who have embraced traditional and functional medicine to do the necessary research and daily work that helps people to stay young and healthy at any age.

Wright

I read that your practice, Élan Anti-Aging and Longevity Center, incorporates alternative and complementary therapies to promote health and youthful aging. What does that mean?

Shelby-Lane

I must start by saying that we are speaking together at a time when the world is focused on going *green*. Going green in medicine is so very do-able. Movies like *SICKO* help a person to see and understand the overall problems we are facing in health care, and the need for prevention, whenever possible. My practice, Élan Anti-Aging and Longevity Center, has been changing over time, and is going green on prevention and wellness therapies. My practice is now part of a certified therapeutic lifestyle program called *FirstLine Therapy*. That means looking at the whole person and managing health conditions by seriously incorporating dietary and lifestyle changes to help reduce the effects of aging and chronic illness and disease. It's more than a facelift or skin care, which is important to the quality of life. My focus is on high energy, mental clarity, full function, and the prevention of disease well into old age. Lifestyle changes can help you self-correct and monitor changes as they occur by using lab and diagnostic studies that are markers for aging, along with health coaching, great nutrition, stress management and self-tracking, I am also incorporating energy medicine modalities that are used to locate and treat difficult cases even after treatment failures. Non-invasive skin enhancement is also part of the practice, as new and better products via research and technology are coming to the forefront. —"Ageless medicine, ageless living" is our motto.

Good health is what everybody wants. I haven't met anyone who doesn't want this one aspect of life—along with more money. But I focus on the wealth of your health. A therapeutic lifestyle program means making decisions and choices every moment of every day that will enhance your health and help prevent disease, enabling you to live a full, healthy and happy life. Helping you make the right choice is how I help.

FirstLine Therapy involves a process of certifying your practice based upon national criteria, and it is based on extensive scientific research, demonstrating that many of the chronic diseases associated with aging can be prevented or even treated by adopting a healthy lifestyle, early and consistently.

We look at a person's medical, social, family, mental, emotional, and environmental background, including their nutritional status, exercise and fitness profile, hormone levels, such as estrogen, testosterone, progesterone, thyroid, and adrenal (stress) hormones, and growth hormone. We look at the hormones that decline as you age. We look at life style issues, toxin exposure, and stress, and we formulate an integrated health profile that helps keep them on track, healthy, and youthful. It's easier to spot problems and course correct with this method. Patients become the leaders of their healthcare program by establishing personal health goals and working with their healthcare providers for technical management.

A FirstLine Therapy therapeutic lifestyle program is now recommended by leading health organizations as the primary therapy for conditions such as cardiovascular disease and diabetes, stress related disorders, fatigue disorders, PMS, menopause, other hormone related symptoms, and conditions related to overweight and obesity. The fundamentals of the program put a person on the path to optimal health through a combination of balanced eating, regular exercise, stress reduction and appropriate/recommended nutritional supplementation, with condition specific nutrients, and sleep for proper mind/body functioning. The program is individualized, which is ideal based on the patient's specific bioelectrical impedance numbers. It includes practitioner consultations, solutions for staying young, simple eating guidelines, progress tracking, lifestyle counseling, and nutritional product recommendations with a certified health coach or lifestyle educator.

This transition to private practice from emergency medicine has been quite a learning experience and a growth challenge, full of financial pitfalls. I literally had to re-invent myself and my thinking. I actually made the transition to this practice by doing disability exams for the State that taught me more about the plight of the health and healthcare of Americans —or the lack of it. The transition has taken seven years. It also taught me how to look at my weaknesses and strengths to become better at what I say and what I do. You must know that I was never taught any of this in medical school or residency.

By reinventing myself, and finding my passion in the field of medicine, I learned how to prevent disease and how to optimize patients' health, so that they can live the maximum life span and beyond to one hundred and twenty years. Of course, this requires starting a prevention program, the earlier, the better, and with consistent effort. This has been fun and exciting work. I'm the medical version of George Forman—and move over, Willard Scott!

Wright

You are said to believe that humor or laughter is good medicine. You are a graduate of Second City Comedy School in Chicago; what did you learn at Second City that applies to medicine?

Shelby-Lane

I spent over $40,000 for my comedy degree, which is a Second City T-shirt (anyone can buy at it Second City for about ten bucks). So, I just learned to laugh at myself. I commuted from Detroit to Chicago by plane twice a week for two years. I knew the entire flight crew by name and schedule. So yes, I graduated from Second City Chicago, where all the great comedians and humorists came from—Gilda Radner, John Belushi, Steve Martin, and many other funny guys and gals. That was the most fun I ever had. I also started my own comedy troupe at the same time called Girlfriend Village & Co., in Detroit. Ronni, (my friend and comedienne) and friends at Girlfriend Village & Co., and I produced and performed over thirty live shows. We had so much fun. I performed as Tina Turner with the Ikettes (Ronni and Marsha), singing Proud Mary. I also performed locally at Mark Ridley's Comedy Castle, and I also took numerous comedy writing and performing courses in California with Gene Peret (Bob Hope's comedy writer). All this was very important work in shaping my comic mind. I hired an acting coach, Bob, and I made a fool of myself on stage. It's called "practice". There's nothing like dying on stage. But I never gave up. That's the incredible part—even to this day, I still take classes with Gene, and I still practice, on stage, in front of an audience.

Laughter is one of those things that is God-given. It's truly a gift. Just having a great sense of humor is a gift. When my best friend, Jackie, was killed, my sister, Sheila, and my husband took me to the comedy club several days later. I laughed and cried at the same time.

I really meet a lot of sad people. They never use their humor. Everyone is born with it; but others are more in tune with it, and others develop it more. Some become great comedians: Jay Leno, Chris Rock, Ellen, Bill Cosby, Eddie Murphy and Whoopi, just to name a few. Some comedians are also very sad and their humor comes from that truth as well. But, I just love to laugh. Making people laugh is hard work, but it's still fun. I created a show called "Laugh Attack: Stopping the Number One Killer: Heart Disease." It included standup and improv comedy. It was important for my audience to understand heart health through laughter—to make the audience learn through laughter.

Many people don't understand this, but we all laugh. In every culture and in any language, people laugh. You always know when someone is happy; I don't care if you're in Asia, Australia, Africa, the U.K. the United States, or Canada, if you look around and someone is laughing, you know that this is the "gift of life." It's so important. You have heard that laughter is the best medicine. Well, I don't want to get sued by *Reader's Digest,* so I'll say, "Laughter is good medicine," and it does work for a lot of things.

Dr. Candace Pert, is a researcher who wrote a book called *The Molecules of Emotion.* She wrote that there are endorphins throughout our entire body—in every cell—not just our brain or nervous system. She is currently doing some fantastic research on HIV disease. The beginning was the "Molecules of Emotion," with laughter and humor, and how good it is for us and good for health.

So Yes, I graduated from Second City Comedy School in Chicago. I'm a standup comedian, I write comedy scripts, I perform as Nurse Ratchitt, and I laugh a lot—mostly at myself.

Wright

You appeared on *The Oprah Winfrey Show* on the topic of "Kids killing kids." Would you tell our readers a little bit about that?

Shelby-Lane

As emergency physician, I saw so many kids dying in the City of Detroit. I also pronounced many of them dead on arrival. Then I looked at the statistics nationwide, and it was just as depressing.

I began working on a project developed by Dr. Prothrow-Stith from Boston—a violence prevention curriculum. I visited Boston and brought the program back to the Detroit Public Schools, training the teachers to put it in our school curriculum. I went on to become part of a film, called *Wasted Dreams.*

The problem of violence is even worse now. But at that point in time, my focus was on violence prevention, thinking that I could make an impact on the situation. So, I appeared on *The Oprah Winfrey Show* talking about the high homicide rate in the City of Detroit regarding kids with guns and kids killing kids. It was a spin-off of other areas of violence prevention and the violence prevention curriculum that I founded in Boston. I was also working on an "adopt a school program" founded by the Thomas Jefferson Center in Pasadena, California. I put a lot of effort into training teachers and working with kids on community work at that time.

When I went on *The Oprah Winfrey Show*, I went with a group of parents called "Save Our Sons and Daughters" founded by Clementine Barfield, who lost her son to violence. I continued working with kids and violence prevention for about ten years and I still do a little bit. I was also appointed as a Clinical Assistant Professor in the Department of Community Medicine at Wayne State University and completed a clinical study in the emergency department at Detroit Receiving Hospital, profiling victims of violent crime who presented to the Emergency Department. Our findings were that 60 percent of the victims we studied knew their assailant.

That was an exciting time to go on Oprah's show and discuss the problem. I wish I had a better solution. It's still a huge problem. The issue was the number of guns and easy access, media violence, and on and on. That was in the late '80s. It has become a different story now, especially with the coming of the Internet. There needs to be more work done in that area of prevention so that our children can grow up to be safe and healthy. There are so many reasons and no simple answers to this epidemic of violence. I think that children's health is a very important issue, now and always.

Wright

It seems to me that your life has been about serving. As a result of your work with youth and teachers you won an award for Women of Distinction in Michigan. What was that all about?

Shelby-Lane

That award stemmed from my work with the Detroit Public Schools and educating the teachers in the Violence Prevention Curriculum and working with SOSAD—Save Our Sons and Daughters. As a result, the women who formed this organization recognized my work and contributions to the community and they gave me an award for being one of the Women of Distinction in Medicine/Michigan. I still have that award. It was an engraved clock—a symbol of time well spent well in serving. As time goes by, I always remember that as a grand moment in time and that was a good thing. I continue to receive other awards but that one was very special because the kids are so special. They are our greatest resource.

Wright

On your radio talk show, *Dr. Shelby-Lane and the Medicine Show,* you have interviewed such notables as the ageless Dick Clark; academy award-winning actor, James Coburn; weight loss guru, Dr. Robert Atkins; and author and motivator Les Brown. In your opinion, is radio and television a good way to reach more people with a serious message or is it simply entertainment?

Shelby-Lane

I don't know if you know the data on health care information and where people get their information, but it's not usually from the doctor in the majority of cases. Most health information is absorbed/acquired from the media. The breakdown is the media, the pharmacist, family and friends, and then the doctor or health care institutions (20 percent). About 40 to 50 percent of the information people get comes from the media. More and more, most people get health information from television, radio, and the Internet. Health care providers have too little time to do patient teaching, so the media is doing the teaching from a variety of sources, some reliable, some not. The next highest percentage comes from local pharmacies and then friends and family.

Once you arrive at the major health care institutions and hospitals, you're on your own. You might see the nurse who is limited in her/his explanation of your condition because of the privacy act that have been set up to help protect you and your privacy from everyone—even those who know you. Once you see the resident (doctor-in-training), he or she is still limited by the attending physician who shows up for several precious minutes of time to talk in medical jargon, known only by the insiders. So, now we're back to television. Since health care has changed so much, you might get five to seven minutes of your doctor's time, at most, in the office or in the hospital. So the media is very important.

In any town or city you will see that there's a health journalist or in some cases now, you will see a media doctor/MD/DO explaining the latest health story. You can also see that the Internet is responsible for a shift in thinking and the cost that people are paying "out of pocket" for health remedies. It is predicted possibly fifty billion dollars are spent for nutritional therapy and treatments. People are getting information from a variety of sources now, which was not even possible in the '70s and '80s. Computer technology, the Internet and the media have changed everything. I'm even involved with an online medical information service, providing direction and recommendations to clients worldwide. I never knew that there was such a need for clarity regarding health issues that could be served via the Internet. People just want clarity and direction, and these folks are always looking for a second or third opinion, even if not in person.

The media outlets have also caused doctors to change their thinking—since there is direct to consumer advertising and patients are more aware and savvy; and they are asking more sophisticated questions. This is good. The doctors and health care providers realize that they must also keep up with the literature as well as media references, worldwide. We live in a vast information world, but we have also shifted to a *recommendation* world. That piece of the puzzle is still missing with any credible consistency.

So, I watch television every day to follow health media info that the public is exposed to, and I frequently get updates on the latest trends in medicine, the latest outbreak, the latest scare or cure, even though I'm usually aware of this far in advance of the media. I've done disaster medical relief work and I provided medical assistance to the victims of Hurricane Katrina. I stayed glued to the television night and day, following the storm and the tragic conditions of the people. I followed the blog being sent from of New Orleans. Then I collected medicines from doctors in Detroit with the help of the Detroit Medical Society, and Drs. Lonnie Joe and Aaron Maddox, and made a solo trip from Detroit to the south to help out. My friend Ernie, who is a nurse, helped along the way.

Media is vital to life and death in many situations. Good reporting makes it so. I attend medical conferences six to eight times a year, but I attend online classes two to three times a week with some of the best and brightest physicians and healthcare providers worldwide, via Webinars and teleseminars. I love the online educational process. Learning from the masters is more important. But the media gives me a vehicle to get the word out to the masses with a different slant. It's a point of view that most people are watching, hearing, and reading. Medical television dramas are also important for telling the stories of life, even if it is stretched a bit.

It was interesting talking with Dick Clark because he had high cholesterol, and as many people know, he eventually had a stroke—one of the complications of cardiovascular disease. I now work with the American Heart Association with their *Go Red for Women* campaign and I am a Power to End Stroke Ambassador. That education was very important.

James Coburn's interview was about his arthritis and using supplements like MSM, Methyl Sulfonyl Methane. He went on to die of a heart attack.

Les Brown is a good friend and a prostate cancer survivor. He was a great guest because of his ability to inspire listeners to change their habits—not an easy challenge. He's a winner.

When you hear entertainers speak about their stories, you frequently discover what you have in common with them. Celebrities are no different than we are. They have the same issues. They teach through their stories and their experiences and we can learn from them. I think they are the glue that can make people listen. People like to listen to celebrities' stories and learn how they are just like us.

Wright

You have described yourself as a perpetual Wannabe. What are you planning and dreaming of doing with your life in the future?

Shelby-Lane

My radio show, *Dr. Shelby-Lane and the Medicine Show*, is now going to be *Dr. Shelby-Lane and the Medicine Show on Internet TV*, and it will hopefully be broadcast on television. I have quite a few celebrities lined up for that. So this was a very good question in terms of celebrities in the past. I'm still using that theme for my show. It is a magazine format show that should be quite interesting.

I am also writing some short, short films that are going to be health related, with a humorous twist. I am also working on a screenplay and a sitcom along with continuing with my private practice. I've also incorporated a corporate wellness program into my online practice, which will allow me to use all of the resources of the Firstline Therapy program I am very, very, very busy. It is all worth it and fun because it all relates to being centered, focused, and authentically living out my passion. It's all health related and emphasizes laughter as good medicine. There is only so much time in the day, (1440 minutes to be exact), but if you are focusing on and doing what you love, you'll find that you have more hours than most to accomplish your goals. Being swamped with too much to do is a problem for most, so I keep a beautiful picture close by that says, "Procrastination is the thief of time".

Wright

You do realize that the subtitle of this book is *The Keys to a Well Balanced Life?*

Shelby-Lane

That is right, and from my point of view, life is well balanced when you have a focus on your passion. I am currently working with a program that has helped me make significant changes because I had to look at all these different things I was doing. The program looks at your Time Quotient. We all have an IQ, and we also have a TQ. God gave us only twenty-four hours in a day and time is the equal opportunity employer.

The program works like this. You complete a questionnaire and once completed you will get a score, which will be your TQ.

My first score was appalling. I was only working at 9 percent of my potential. Although a "successful doctor" I was failing in areas that I had read about for years in over four hundred self-help books. I spoke to the owners of the program, "ER & Kent," and they helped me to understand where I had weaknesses and imbalances. I asked for coaching. (I had already studied health coaching to become a certified Health Coach, in addition to everything else I've been doing.) I knew coaching was important, but I didn't know how important it was to success. I initially planned to do group coaching for my clients. But I wasn't really ready to do any coaching when I completed the yearlong course. I needed some coaching myself first.

I now have my own personal life coach. This has made a tremendous difference in my success and my ability to "see" and get things done. As I said, I had read over four hundred self-help books and I wanted to know why I was still having difficulty making the necessary changes to become the huge success that I believed I could be. I wanted to know how to stop the small failures and get on with living a successful life. This program helped me to discover that; it helped me to change, it helped me to move forward and look at specific areas of my life with a systematic approach, along with all the other positive thinking that I had been doing for years. They did the math.

Once you complete your test and get a mathematical analysis of who you are, what you're doing, what you're not doing, what you should and could be doing better, where you're failing and why you're successful, what your weaknesses are, then you see it—you'll understand the math. I love math. The "science" of achieving was in my face. The change came with getting a coach who was also trained in this system.

I think (and hope) medicine will change to include this sort of format, with health coaching or some sort of coaching paradigm. It will take time, but the consumer will probably come to demand it. When you look at winning teams like Coach Riley, and his winning basketball team, they usually have great coaches. My coach, Maikel Bailey, is incredible. The universe sent me this great person because it knew I had a need—a need for balance. It has just been a real blessing in my life to understand where I was out of balance and how to get back into balance, living with a real focus along with passion. It has meant letting a lot of other things go. I also had the help of a professional organizer, the Organized Happy Helper, Debbe Tebbe and my cohorts/friends, Millicent, Ann, Sheryl & Barbara to help get me back on track. What a pushy team. But, that's what is needed to get thongs done. Letting go is the first step for some. But the TQ system helps you identify where you are and the actual steps (10) needed to make a successful change and leap forward. You have to be able let a whole lot go—a lot. It doesn't sound as though I let a whole lot go, but I actually have. I get many offers, invitations, and requests every day, along with distractions and personal tragedies. At this point in my life the answer is, "On [to my real passion] and No [to the soft stuff]." This is an acronym that stands for balance: ONNO. I disappear a lot now. I also sleep more than I dance now, and dancing is my first passion. I love to dance. I'll be dancing again soon—the Salsa, merengue, rumba, mambo, and the tango.

Wright

After many years of experience in their chosen field, many people of distinction elect to speak, train, and consult in order to help more people. Are you considering speaking as a career?

Shelby-Lane

I've done quite a bit of professional speaking in my life. I plan to do more speaking in the near future, and I am always open to speaking/teaching. My first college degree was in education/teaching. I love speaking, especially to kids and parents and professional groups. My current emphasis is on health coaching, both individuals and groups. I am currently conducting teleseminars, and I have a series of twelve lectures on healthy living and staying young. I also have an *ASK the Doctor* website, which guides me on the issues that people need answers to in a very quick and easy format. I also speak on issues that are currently plaguing American health, in particular, such as heart disease and obesity, and the problems associated with chronic diseases—heart disease, diabetes, cancer, and stroke prevention. In addition, I am speaking with human resources at corporations to help develop and implement corporate wellness programs, which involves conducting a lunch and learn program for the staff.

Wright

In closing what would you say to our readers to help them live a more healthy better and more fulfilling life?

Shelby-Lane

Here is a list:

The six most common things a person wants from health are the following: Something for energy, something for pain, some thing for sleep, something for stress, something for sex and now, something for weight. These are primarily quality of life issues, and very important, although not life threatening. Most illnesses and states of health will revolve around these issues, no matter what the presenting problems. Looking at lifestyle, stressors, and diet, nutritional, and environmental factors is very important in the health care equation.

Guidelines for Better Health: Specifically, wellness is a state in which a human being functions at an optimal level, body, mind, and spirit. Giving gratitude for your health, whatever it is, starts and maintains the process for health and healing. In general, I currently follow a therapeutic lifestyle program implemented by Firstline Therapy for my clinic and patients that I think will benefit anyone.

You must expect/visualize and imagine better health for yourself and take the steps to execute your best health program, now and into the future (fifteen years or so).

Set current and future goals. This may include yearly and regular checkups with a qualified complementary and integrative medicine expert as a good first choice.

Health coaching is a very useful option to help maintain and monitor goals and health challenges/changes. This should be done by someone who understands the stages of change, along with healthy aging and prevention and the diagnostic tests that give you the best bang for your buck.

Routine tests for healthy aging have been re-defined. Living to be one hundred with a healthy "mind, body, and spirit" is the new *norm.*

Get yearly physical exams for maintenance checks with the appropriate blood, urine, and diagnostic screening tests, as indicated for your age and sex and past medical history. More frequent exams and studies may be indicated.

Yes, see your doctor on your birthday. You should give yourself the gift of a yearly health exam on your birthday.

1. Diet: You will always benefit from an "anti-inflammatory and low glycemic index" diet, with foods such as fruits, whole grains, vegetables, and low glycemic index

carbohydrates. Make an effort to eliminate all processed foods, if possible. Eat breakfast.

2. Moderate exercise: (increased physical activity), relaxation, and stress reduction should be included daily. This should include interval training with resistance exercises so that you can gradually increase your activity to optimal levels.

3. Detoxification program: This will help rid your body of environmental toxins that bombard you on a daily basis. (See the *National Geographic,* October 2006 issue regarding toxins.)

4. Nutritional Supplementation: Digestive enzymes, vitamins, minerals, vitamin D, and omega three fatty acids are helpful in reducing inflammatory changes and improving your memory. Many companies offer high quality supplements. I prefer vitamin and mineral testing so that an individualized and specific supplement can be created just for you.

5. Cardiovascular profile: This includes methods to determine risk factors for heart disease and possible sudden cardiac death. You should know your risk factors and know your numbers. Non-invasive tests offer a first line of detection. The American Heart Association has multiple programs to help with diet, lifestyle, exercise, and community events.

6. Never smoke and if you do, quit. Avoid smokers and smoke-filled environments.

7. Bio-identical hormone replacement testing and therapy with balancing will help to keep you youthful, but only if you are a candidate for this form of therapy. Follow up testing must be done by a qualified professional to maintain balance.

8. Stress reduction, relaxation, visualization, and laughter. Support for emotional health is a must for great health. Get enough sleep.

9. Cancer screening profiles can help with early detection. Multiple screening tests exist for the ongoing detection of cancer and they are usually organ specific based upon age,

gender, presenting symptoms, family history and environmental exposure. Your doctor can determine the best tests to be done.

10. Drink purified water, preferably distilled or purified and not tap water.

11. Bioelectrical Impedance Analysis (BIA): BIA testing helps to determine body composition, basal metabolic rate, water, fat, and muscle mass and intracellular and extracellular water ratios, as a measure of cellular health and toxicity.

12. Energy medicine is a new field of treatment done via pulse biofeedback from a company that is seeking FDA approval. This is very exciting.

I have several closing thoughts and recommendations: I borrowed this formula for change from my friends and coaches (Alex Mandossian, in particular). In summary, they have encouraged me to ask the following questions.

Five questions to ask yourself about making a change in your health/life:

1. What is your pain or problem? What is your health problem(s)? Clearly define this answer for yourself, with or without a doctor. What you are suffering from, what do you need to improve or change about your health. Define and understand what is your pain, your problem, your health challenge or your health desire.

2. Next, what is the resolution of this problem? How will you solve it or attempt to solve it? What do you want to do, or what are you willing to do to solve the problem? What are the possible resolutions of this problem? Doctors, health care professionals, health insurance, physical and mental, diagnostic tests, therapy, drugs, nutritionals, lifestyle, diet, exercise, alternative therapies, second opinions, friends and family, etc. Look for a resolution with an eye on the target goal.

3. Why are you stuck? What is the resistance, internal (fear) vs. external (the system, etc,)? Write a page or two to help you clearly define the reason you feel stuck.
4. What is the process for making change? How do you get unstuck? What is the resolution process? Your own health care system will help you to discover the answer via methods such as health coaching, counseling, second opinions, and groups with similar situations. Find someone who has gone through a similar situation and found success to help understand the process. Look for mentors and coaches who have already cracked the code, so to speak.
5. What is my first step? Physical action, according to David Allen. Make a list, a Journal. Move. Baby step by baby step. Action by action according to your list.

I believe in being proactive about health care. I think that you need to establish who is on your personal health team. You must decide who is on your team. Healthcare now operates in systems. If you go into any city you will find a health care system such as the Mayo Clinic Health System, Detroit Medical Center, Henry Ford Health Care System, and University of Michigan Health Care Systems. Health care is now taking a systems approach. When you enter a hospital, you become a patient with a number in the system. Therefore, you want to look at creating your own personal health care system. What does that include? You are the head of your health care system. You need to have a copy your medical records. You need to know your medical history and have a complete medical profile. This helps especially if you have a sudden illness or have been injured.

The privacy act, which is called the Health Insurance Portability and Accountability Act (HIPAA), makes it harder for doctors and specialists to access your medical information. It protects you and your privacy but it makes it harder for doctors to access and share information about you. Therefore, it is really important that you keep your medical records.

If you have a medical professional in your family who can help you, that would be great. Sometimes you don't understand what doctors are talking about. We doctors talk in an odd language and very fast. If you can get a doctor to explain your condition to you, and talk with you (instead of at you) or with someone in your family, that is great.

You need a food coach, a health coach, and a fitness trainer/buddy. Put your grocer on your health care team. If you can't afford these folks, then become and stay active. Join a group. It's cheaper by the dozen. Always read labels. It is even more important, as we age, to get a better understanding of food and food ingredients. When it comes to diet and nutrition, eat organic as often as possible. Chew your food forty times before swallowing—just as your mom may have told you.

All of these recommendations are easily doable and affordable and, as stated above, they can be done in group sessions. There are so many free things in America, but many of us don't take advantage of them. Wal-Mart has been traveling around the country and for $229 you can have a non-invasive scan of your body for heart prevention. This would otherwise cost $2,300 at the local health care system and that's only if your insurance provider approved it after your doctor ordered it—not likely. Preventive screening and diagnostic tests are extremely important in health care prevention.

Stay abreast of the latest trends and diagnostic tools in healthcare, especially the non-invasive modes. I am investing in an energy medicine device developed in Germany, which is currently undergoing clinical trials and studies in pain management throughout the United States. It made discovery about my health, which was previously confirmed by an MRI.

Watch television news and understand health news and try to determine what and who is a credible and reliable source. Use the Internet as part of your health care system. Always, always ask questions from your health care providers. Get a second and even a third opinion.

Make sure you avoid processed foods, MSG, and artificially sweetened beverages. Understand food allergies as a source of unrecognized illnesses. Many people are unknowingly sensitive to gluten and wheat products as a cause for their ongoing and unrecognized illness.

Have fun, relax, and go out with the family. My family is my biggest support team including the kids (Brandon (Stephanie), Lindsay, Ross, and my grandkids). Chill out, be thankful, de-stress, sing, and dance. Dance in the kitchen. Go on vacation. See the world. Stay open-minded. Forgive and then forget . . . well, if you can't forget, then at least forgive. I also wake up and listen to the radio with MOJO in the Morning for phone scams and humor, on radio 95.5. They make my day. And remember to dream—dream big. My big dream is to dance and to "fall" on national television on Dancing with the Stars.

There are some basic, easy things that don't even require the help of a doctor. People are spending large sums of money, out of pocket for complementary and integrative therapy and answers to their health care problems.

Keep a spiritual balance in all that you do. Emotional health is taken for granted and stress is mounting in every family. Keep a journal. Meditate and pray every day. With regenerative medicine, you regenerate your mind—you redesign your health care plan for yourself, you create your own system, and you decide that you are the head coach along with your doctor. You must take responsibility for every action in your life. Being healthy, wealthy, and streetwise requires serious personal choices. And on that note, I'd like to thank my entire team, including my family, at home, at work (Sierra), and at church (Rev. Bill, etc.), along with my friends and support staff for their patience, love, and understanding.

Wright

What an interesting conversation, especially the last question. I am positive you have given our readers a lot to think about.

I really appreciate the time you've spent with me this morning and answering all these questions. I know that you are a very busy lady and I commend you for all the great work that you are doing.

Shelby-Lane

Thank you. As you know, it does take time, energy, and passion; but it's all focused and balanced and I've enjoyed it immensely.

Wright

Today we have been talking with Cynthia Shelby-Lane, MD, who is also known as the Ageless Doctor. She practiced emergency medicine for over twenty-three years. Her experience in dealing with life and death crises in that venue allowed her to see and realize the limitations of traditional medicine, which led her to seek methods of prevention.

Cynthia, thank you so much for being with us in *Getting Things Done, Keys to a Well Balanced Life.*

About the Author

"Laughter is Good Medicine," says Cynthia Shelby-Lane, MD. She is a doctor, speaker, comedienne, and talk show host who loves to laugh. Do you know a doctor, who stops to save a life, then gets up on stage to make you laugh . . . at life . . . at yourself . . . and at herself? Well, Shelby-Lane, MD, is that kind of doctor. Known as "the Ageless Doctor," Shelby-Lane is a graduate of the University of Michigan Medical School. She trained as a surgeon at the University of Texas in Houston and committed herself to saving lives as an emergency physician in Detroit. She then re-invented herself and is now a board-certified, anti-aging specialist, keeping people young and healthy from the inside out.

Her practice, Élan Anti-Aging & Longevity Center, incorporates alternative and complementary therapies to promote optimal health and youthful aging. She also expanded her practice to the Internet as "The Internet Doctor," answering questions for patients worldwide through a detailed Internet evaluation. The doctor is also a certified, professional health coach, conducting monthly teleseminars, and helping people make difficult health and life choices and create changes for optimum health and wellness. Shelby-Lane has also established a Corporate Wellness Program. She and her staff work with the company's Human Resources department to help develop and implement a lifestyle assessment and lifestyle modification program to help keep their employees healthy, and reduce health care and insurance costs.

Seen on national radio and television, discussing issues such as anti-aging, heart disease, weight loss, stress reduction, and cancer, Shelby-Lane speaks nationwide and is also a certified professional health coach. She tackles tough social issues through community work and took thousands of dollars worth of drugs and medical supplies to the victims of Katrina on a solo mission in 2005.

This graduate of Second City Comedy School in Chicago and student at UCLA Motion Picture and Television Program produces television shows and a "live" comedy show called, "Laugh Attack: Stopping the Number One Killer—Heart Disease.

Appearances on *The Oprah Winfrey Show* and featured articles in the *New York Times, Ebony,* and *Jet* magazines and *Women's Health Style* magazine have given her expert status as the anti-aging and comedy doc. She can cook, too. She's no Emeril or Rachel Ray, but Dr. Shelby-Lane is now the host of her new food show, *What's Cookin', Doc?* Trading in her stethoscope for an apron, her food show features "food remedies and foods that heal." for an extreme health makeover. So, if "Laughter is Good Medicine," then "great food is the cure."

Cynthia Shelby-Lane, MD   800-584-4926
19785 W. 12 Mile Road, Suite 293   agelessdoctor@aol.com
Southfield, Michigan 48076   www.shelbylaneMD.com